Paths We Choose

Give Thanks for Life's Lessons
Memories Made
&
Times Shared

& R Walters May 21/13

By George Walters

Also By
George Walters

****

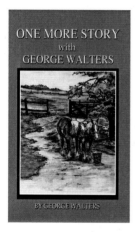  

Published 2011

ISBN: 978-0-9809884-3-7

Coming Soon

His First
Never Before Published
Novel

The Long Road Home

The last two stories in this book gives the readers a glimpse of what the Long Road Home will be like; showing his style and how folks got things done.

You'll meet railroaders, card sharks, cattlemen and women and men of yesteryear.

So look for the Long Road Home and come along, as George recaptures, the humor, violence and adventure of the great Canadian and American frontier. You'll be glad you did.

Paths We Choose

George Walters

Illustrations by Ruth Walters

Ruth Walters is an artist with a vision. Her self taught skills are a rare taste which brings folks back to an era in time, that most never see.

Her sketches at the beginning of each story gives the reader a glimpse of what George's stories entails without words.

She is able to bring the very remote past up to the present giving it a place in todays world with meaning, love and kindness.

Her expertise is that of a surgeon, as with each stroke of her brush or pen, life begins to flourish.

A very talented lady.

Acknowledgments

My deepest thanks goes out to my wife Ruth, my two sons, Craig & Karl and my Daughter-In-Law Krista, for their help and support. Also all the newspapers, magazines and book stores that have helped in the promotion of all my books.

In fairness to everyone this time around, attributes were not added to this book, as there were just too many. But many thanks goes out to those that have called, E-mail & wrote me, not to forget all those that have taken the time to come to my book signings, as it is great to meet you all personally.

It is you, my readers that keeps me writing.

This Book Is Dedicated To

My Wife Ruth, My Sons
Craig & Karl
Our Daughter-In-Law Krista
Our Grandson Cole, along with all the Grandchildren that I am sure
will follow.
&
Nancy, Daughter of Reg and Laura

Also In Memory Of
Reg, Laura, Grey Wolf, My Dad Earl
My Grandmother and Grandfather
Margret and George

Table of Contents

Table Of Contents

Table Of Contents

Preface

George Walters lives with his lovely wife Ruth in the small town of Port Loring, Ontario, Canada.

His stories skip around from place to place as he reflects back to his early days on the dairy farm in Coldwater, Ontario, with Reg and Laura Potter. They were an older couple that raised him from the age of five until he was a teenager. His Dad then brought him home to live in Beamsville, on the fruit farm.

As his memories and imaginations come to him, his stories are put down on paper. You will feel you are right there experiencing it all...as his life unfolds.

George's extended family of readers have come to know and love him through his easy, down to earth way he portrays his message.

These stories are fascinating and light-hearted accounts of life in the Rural communities that bring back fond memories of years gone by. His gentle and insightful recollections take us back to our roots. With honesty, humor and caring philosophy, he generously shares his thoughts with you.

As he reflects back to the moments in time as a young boy the stories bring back the simple life, the values of family, respect, pride in ones self and the hard work our forefathers endured to make this country what it is today.

These stories are part of our inheritance. Read them and pass them on to the next generation.
His first three books have been winners among his readers and have encouraged him to write another.

I hope you enjoy this book as well, and you become one of his extended family too.

"Enjoy, Paths We Choose"

A book everyone can take pleasure in, young and old, and rekindle the experiences of the past that are long being forgotten.

Wisdom

Many years ago I remember Grey Wolf saying to me. George, when all seems lost, become your enemy.

Never were words so well chosen that can take a man, woman or child out of a state of despair, letting them rise above all those that think that they are right and you are wrong.
*****

Being Indian is mainly in your heart. It's a way of walking with the earth instead of upon it. A lot of the history books talk about us Indians in the past tense, but we don't plan on going anywhere...We have lost so much, but the thing that holds us together is that we all belong to and are protectors of the earth; that's the reason for us being here. Mother Earth is not a resource, she is an heirloom.
*****

Children are the seeds of our future. Plant love in their hearts and water them with wisdom and life's lessons.
When they are grown, give them space to grow.
*****

You must never dwell on sadness and never look in dark corners.
*****

Search for yourself. Do not allow others to make your path for you. It is your road and yours alone. Others may walk it with you but none can walk it for you.
*****

The negative energy that you put out into the universe will multiply when it returns to you.
*****

You cannot nurture and help others if you cannot nurture and help yourself first.
*****

Only by listening closely to the language of Nature can you learn her secrets.

Paths We Choose

By George Walters

George enjoys hearing from his readers.
He may be contacted at:
stories@keepingnotes.com

Early Risers

Years ago there was one thing that was usually handed down from family to family. "Being an early riser."

When I first moved to the dairy farm it took a few weeks to get my internal clock adjusted to Reg and Laura's ways, *they were the folks that raised me.*

Reg he was always up before daylight and Laura wasn't far behind. Reg would get the old wood stove perkin' and the coffee pot was set over the flame. I would have to say that the smell of the coffee perking away on the stove helped in my getting up, as the aroma would be the first thing to greet me every morning.

Laura used to say, "up and at 'em George, the early bird gets the worm." Reg, he would say, "come on get out of that sack, we are burning daylight." Couldn't figure that out I told him, as there is no daylight to be seen....when we get up.

I didn't get to drinking coffee for a few years as Laura said it would stunt my growth, but I got the next best thing, hot chocolate. I have to say she sure had a knack of making it taste good. Never could figured out the recipe she used totally, but kind of think it had to do with using fresh cream right from our cows. While Reg and I got into our drinks Laura was busy getting things ready for milking. Once done we headed on over to the barn and about half way through our milking Laura got to separating the milk using our old hand crank separator.

1

Soon as she finished that up, she got busy making breakfast and I have to say by that time we were sure a hungry pair.

Another good saying that Laura used to say when it came to getting up early, was.....Early to bed, Early to rise, Makes a fellow, Healthy, Wealthy and Wise.

The early to bed part was no problem for me, as after a hard days work I was ready for it.

Early to rise, well as I said earlier, my internal clock had been put into place.

Healthy, yes, I would have to say our energy source of life has surely looked after me in that department. Oh.....I had a few things go wrong here and there, but for most parts so far I am doing OK.

Wealthy, well I don't know if I could really say I was wealthy, but in some ways I suspect I am. Meaning money wise we always got by, but as my wife has always said, the cupboards always had food in them and the young ones never went to bed hungry and she was always provided for.

On the wise part, well there again I am pretty pleased with the knowledge that I have been given and sure enjoy sharing it with folks that will listen.

One other saying that Laura used a lot always brought a smile to my face. "There is no snooze button on a cat who wants breakfast." And I got to tell ya we sure had a pile of them, should say a barn full, and come milking time it sounded like a choir out there.

Yep it was a good time to be alive living on the farm and each morning I was given a new day. A day that was just waiting for me to make my mark. I have always figured that if one gets up early and gets an early start on the day, good things just have to follow.

Even today I still find myself getting out of bed just before sunrise, not that I have to anymore, but something inside me just can't let me miss the breaking of dawn. I guess some things just stay with a feller over the years huh?

Helpful Hints-To Purify Cistern Water. Cistern Water can be purified by hanging a bag of charcoal in the water.

A Quiet Night In
A Quiet Town

"It was a hot day thinking back," said my Grandfather. "Should say darn hot, and the train I was taking to a friends place in the north sure didn't help matters any. It was suppose to be a half a days trip, but ended up being a whole day and by the time we arrived at my destination it was close to midnight.

On arriving I moved to get off the train handing my stub to the fellow that looks after the tickets, then stepping down onto the platform that led up to the train station. Once off I looked around and found there wasn't another sole to be found. It was a dark night and felt like rain in the air. Fog had settled in over the land around the station and the old lamp which hung on the wall sure didn't put out much light. I walked over to the door and tried to open it, but it was locked tight. A sign on the door read, "we got to sleep sometime, so come back in the morning."

I looked around a bit and way off in the distance I spotted a wee glimmer of a light showing itself now and then. Well no use standing here I thought and headed off to where I seen the light, hoping it might be a house or something.

Well it took me the better part of a half hour to get there and sure enough it was an old cabin and on the window ledge a candle was

3

burning away. I walked over to the house and knocked on the door. No one came for the longest time, so I knocked again. Then from inside a voice came through the door."

"Who is it? If your up to no good and going to cause me trouble I want you to know, I have a loaded shot gun in here just waiting for folks like yourself."

"Nope, don't mean you no harm Sir. Just got off the train here in town and you were the only place I could see that had a light on. Was hoping that you might have a place that I could spend the night, that's out of the weather."

With that the door opened and a man wearing an old torn pair of wool trousers, with a white cotton shirt stood there holding an old double barrel shot gun. Well don't stand there like a darn fool, come on in and close the door. Cold night out there and I am not up to heating the whole outside."

I eased my way around the old shot gun making sure I didn't jar it any, as he had both hammers pulled back and his fingers on the trigger.

"You can put that old gun of yours down mister." I said, "I don't mean you no harm." With that I pulled a half broken chair out from the corner and sat down.

"How come your up this time of night?" The old feller asked.

"Well the train had some problems and, well here I am about five hours late. Sure glad you opened up for me, as it would have been a cool night out there sleeping under a tree."

"I got a pot of coffee sittin' there on the stove if you would like a cup?"

"Sure would," I replied, "love one, haven't had a drink or anything to eat all day."

"I suppose I could rustle you up some eggs, if you like, that's about all I got that's quick to make at this time of night. Guess should say morning."

With that he leaned the old gun up against the wall and proceeded to make me something to eat.

"Live here all alone old timer?" I asked.

"Yep do now. Wife passed on a few days ago. Had what they called consumption. Wasn't nice the last while before she left. Sure was hard on her, but I am thinkin' she is better off."

"Guess that is why you have a candle burning in the window huh?" I asked.

"Yep sure is, you....know they say if you burn a candle in the window for five nights after a loved one passes on that the light from the candle will show them where they are suppose to go. Well that's

what I have been doing and so far, darn my luck, I haven't seen my lovely Mary."

Well we talked for a bit longer I ate and then he handed me a blanket saying I could stretch out over there in the corner.

"All I can offer you son."

"Better than the alternative," I replied.

I laid there for a short time and then half dosed off, awaking to a noise over by the stove. To my surprise, I noticed a woman with an apron on standing there kind of lookin' at me in a strange way. She has wispy white hair with a corn cob pipe clamped between her teeth. She didn't say anything, kind of just stared at me. Gave me an eerie feeling for a minute. I turned over and got up. Looking back, the lady was gone. Well I'll be darned I thought, I could have sworn I seen a woman standing there.

A few minutes later my moving around woke up the old feller and we got to talking. I told him what I had seen, and he said. "Don't you be tellin' me no lies young feller, as I just as soon shoot ya as look at ya."

I then told him what she looked like, with her corn cob pipe in her mouth. With them few words the old feller sat down at the table, and started to cry.

"That's my Mary," he said. "That's her for sure. Guess she found her way home. Well....young feller, I am glad you dropped by now, as at least she had some company, with me sleepin' and all, I look forward to talkin' to her again."

With that I said my good byes with thanks, shook the old fellers hand noticing the tears in his eyes, and left.

Before leaving I looked back at the candle in the window, almost burned to the bottom. "Who would have thought," I said.

"Lots of things like that have happened to me George. That was just one of them."

Helpful Hints-To Preserve Eggs. One quart of salt, one pint of slacked lime and three gallons of fresh water. This will keep eggs for years.

A Day Of Learning

"There is really only one thing that has meaning in ones life, young one."

"What's that?" I asked.

It was a Saturday afternoon midsummer. I had finished my chores and was thinking of going fishing, when Laura the lady of the house asked if I would take a loaf of home made bread that she had just made back to my friend Grey Wolf. He was a great man in my eyes while growing up and a lot of my learnings came directly from him.

"Would be happy to," I replied, " soon as I saddle up Jennie I will be right with you, I can go fishing another day."

With that I called Jennie as she was out in the field and in an instant she was by my side. A few short minutes later I had her saddled up and we were off. Grey Wolf is sure going to enjoy this bread I thought as I rode along.

Thing I liked the most about Grey Wolf was that he was full of information and if asked would gladly share his views on things. Being a young feller at the time, well I sure had a lot of questions that needed answers to and he was always there for me.

The ride back to his cottage was always a pleasant trip as Jennie knew exactly where to go, which left my mind the freedom to wonder onto other things that were at hand at that moment.

Arriving at the cottage I spotted Grey Wolf sitting in his rocking chair on the front porch. I waved as I got nearer and he waved back saying. "What brings you out here on a day that was made for fishing?"

"Well I was going to go fishing but Laura asked if I would bring you this loaf of home made bread out to you, still warm too as I wrapped it up in one of Jennie's blankets before I left."

"For a young fellow to give up his fishing day to bring me a loaf of bread is a man of values, get down and set a spell. While walking the other day I came upon a hive of bees and managed to scoop out a pot of fresh honeycomb. I was wondering what I could use it on, you answered that question, be right back."

I did and pulled up an old box which sat along side his chair.

After a short while of nothing being said, *as our mouths were too full*, Grey Wolf then broke the silence and got to asking me about how things have been going.

"Oh fine I suppose, the teacher at school though, says I need to pay more attention to what is happening around me, as one can learn from all kinds of things."

"Well there young one, her words are wise and it would be of a great advantage to you if you listened and took notice of what was happening around you a bit more."

"I am not sure though what she means by paying more attention to the things around me."

With that Grey Wolf pulled my box up closer to his chair and pointed out to the Crow that was flying overhead.

"See that crow flying above them trees young one? That crow teaches you cleverness, as he is about the smartest of all the birds when it comes to getting things done, without being caught or hurt. Over there on that branch sitting so quietly at this moment, do you see that Jay bird?"

"Yep, I see him and your right, he is being pretty quiet, as usually he is really noisy."

"That Jay young one can teach you a lot about courage. That Jay will take it upon himself to drive off a Hawk ten times his size if he enters his territory. He is able to eliminate fear from his thinking when it comes to standing up for what is right or from those that are trying to take what is his? At night we can also learn, as one just has to watch the crafty owl. From him we learn patience, as he can sit for hours without blinking an eye, his reward is a feast to be enjoyed, patience is well needed in ones life, which most don't have.

The one that is most appreciated in my eyes though young one, is the chickadee. He can not be subdued, he is untamable, invincible, he is wild and has an incredible spirit which tops all others of his kind."

In hearing all this you should now know that you and me have to care for our forests, so that our children, grandchildren and children yet to be born can enjoy and learn as you have. We also have to

7

protect the forests for those that can't speak for themselves, like the birds, animals, fish and trees."

Everything on the earth has a purpose, every disease has a herb or plant to cure that disease growing close by, and every person a mission. This is the native theory of existence young one and you would be wise to heed these words."

"So....do you understand now what your teacher was trying to say?"

"Yes, I think so, that one can learn if he just takes the time to notice what is happening around him."

"Exactly, my friend and you have vision. I have seen that vision that lays inside you. You see things where others do not, that is a gift in itself.

One last thing on the meaning of life, these are not my words, but they are good words, worthy for your ears and mind to dwell on through your journey of life.

"I think over again of all my small adventures through life, my fears, those small ones that seemed so big.

For all the vital things I had to get and reach, and yet, there is only one great thing, the only thing, is to live to see the great day that dawns, and the light that fills the world."

As the day wore on Grey Wolf's words filled my mind, a day of learning, which has stayed with me and will stay with me, till the light of day is never seen again.

Helpful Hints-To Kill Insects Such As, Bedbugs, Moths, Etc.

Hot alum water is the best thing known to destroy insects. Boil it in water till it is dissolved; then apply the hot solution with a brush to closets, bedsteads, cracks or where ever insects are found. All creeping insects may be destroyed by its use. There is no danger of poisoning and its persistent use, will rid you of all the pests.

Borrowing & Loaning

Back in my early days living on the farm I still can hear Laura saying. "George, one thing we don't do here in this house is borrow things from neighbors."

Now in saying that however, every once in awhile we did borrow some things, like maybe if our plow broke down Reg might ask for the loan of the neighbors up the road aways. Just till ours was fixed mind ya and that was usually done right quick too. Should also say here, that before the plow went back to its owner, it would be cleaned up and a new edge would have been put on the blades.

Laura now, she didn't believe in borrowing things, as it brought shame on the family, but everyone has an emergency now and then and when that happened I was sent out to fetch back what ever was needed. But for most parts I would have to say here that Laura and Reg were very self efficient folks. I can't rightly remember ever seeing our cupboards empty, or wanting for things. Not that we had a whole lot of money as we surely didn't, just that we grew most of what we needed and stored it away. I would have to say if any borrowing would be seen around our place, it would be the neighbors borrowing off us.

Occasionally though a cup of sugar might be needed in Laura's department and I would be sent up the road. Laura not only believed borrowing brought shame to the family, she also believed that if you

borrowed say a half of cup of sugar that when returned you make darn sure you sent back a full cup. Or if you borrowed a full cup, you sent back a cup and a half. In other words if you borrowed something, always send it back with more than what you borrowed to begin with, that way the shame is lifted from the families good name. Guess that is why before Reg sent the borrowed plow back to its owner he sharpened the edge on the blades.

Today though things are done a lot different. I have found that borrowing things has become a natural thing to do in ones life.

For myself I never got into borrowing things, might say I did without rather than borrow. I guess that shame Laura talked so much about kind of hung in the back of my mind.

I remember one time I loaned my tractor to the feller down the road from me. He had just moved into our neck of the woods and was trying to get his newly bought farm in shape. I didn't really like the idea of loaning it, but with the folks being new to the area, well....I kind of felt maybe it would be OK.

Another reason would be that, most farmers or folks in farming get to know their equipment. They get to know how to start it just by the sound it makes. Like mine, I give it a bit of choke till it pops, then push the choke back in, turn it over and it starts right up. Or say if one is working in the fields, over the years one knows the sound of the engine when it is running properly, but when something is going wrong one can just seem to sense it, and stops things to have a look. But new folks that don't know these things, well....they keep on working the piece of equipment and that's where problems arise, which sometimes can be quite expensive. Which leads back to my loaning of my tractor.

What happened was I told him about noon to check the oil and make sure it was topped up, as being a bit old it burned a wee bit more than it should. Well this fellow just shrugged it off and didn't check it, working it steadily all day. Ended up the motor ceased up and I had to do a motor job on it before I could get back to my own work.

I knew it would need one sooner or later, but with me using it I wouldn't have had to do it till fall, when things weren't so busy. The other thing that bothered me was this fellow didn't seem to be upset about what had happened. All he said was, darn sorry about the tractor, didn't offer to help me fix it or anything.

I got it fixed OK, just took me the better part of the week to rebuild the motor working late into a few evenings.

Thinking back though if that would have happened, say to Reg, well it would have been fixed and sent back running better than before it was loaned to him. Would have been unheard of just sending it back broken down. Today though things are done differently that's for

sure, and I guess that is why for most parts I got away from loaning things. Especially with the fellow up the road, never loaned him anything anymore. But I can't say I stopped loaning things all together though, as every now and then I have a weak moment. The only thing I do differently when that happens is, I sort of psych myself up for what might happen and live with it.

And who says us older fellers don't change their ways anymore.

Helpful Hints-To Remove The Smell Of Onions From Your Breath.
Parsley eaten with vinegar will destroy the unpleasant breath, caused by eating onions.

Family & Things

For quite a few years now I have had so many folks ask me my feelings on life, family and my views on different things. Well, I have been hesitant in doing so, but after years of being asked I have decided to say a few words on behalf of all those that have asked. Remember now, these are my words and my feelings, along with a few good old time sayings.

Over the years I have found that family members are a pretty important factor in a person's life. Now in saying that I don't mean that one has to like everyone in his or her family.

I remember years ago my old Dad saying, "George one thing you got to remember, you have no way of choosing your family, they are just there."

That is so true, as there is some that I get along with and some I don't. Some I see on a regular basis and some I don't. Some I have to put up with, some I don't. I figure it this way. If anyone happens to come in between my wife or our young ones, I just don't associate with them, simple as that.

For example, the powers that be. I don't have anything against any one man or woman that works for them, but I don't have to associate myself with them, if I so choose. There is a few though that I let talk.

On the subject of powers that be, here is another old saying I like a lot and is so true.

"Remember, that a government big enough to give you everything you want, is also big enough to take away everything you have."

I guess what I am saying is, the world has changed in the way it looks at things, but for myself, I am still the same and probably always will be. Reason being, I have built my life around my beliefs and they have done me and my family well for as long as I can remember, so I would be a fool to change my ways now. But to each their own I always say.

I have had a lot of good friends throughout my day, I can say that for certain and I have always respected others points of view, right or wrong. In general I have supported family values and principles, not human beings and looking back it has served me well.

I know there is some that put their family ahead of everything and anyone and they are entitled to do that. They build their whole life around family members which is OK too, if that's the road you choose to follow. Myself I believe every one should pick the road wisely in the beginning and then follow it relentlessly. Some do, some don't.

Some of my roads where chosen for me in the early days until I became a man, then I choose the road to follow that I wanted. I made mistakes no doubt, but mistakes are OK, as long as one learns by them.

But I can say this, the roads I took are from my choosing and mine alone and I have never felt regret in those I chose. My family has followed me throughout their younger years until they were men and I never once tried to sway them away from the road of their choice. If asked about a problem and I have been through a similar situation, I then would tell them how I overcame it. Then I leave it up to them, as it is not for me to make up their minds.

I can honestly say I have raised my family to have minds of their own and I am real proud of the way they have chosen to lead their lives. I don't think there can be any better rewards in life, than to sit back and look out at ones sons or daughters and see them enjoying life doing what they love.

Yep times has changed and I for one think a lot has gone wrong throughout my time here on this old earth and it's too bad too. I can honestly say though that I have done all I can to make this world a better place and my conscience is clear. The problems the old world has now, lies in the fault of others. Something to think about.

Helpful Hints-To Remove Wrinkles. Melt and stir together one ounce of white wax, two ounces of strained honey, and two ounces of juice from Lilly bulbs; apply to the face every night, it is said that your wrinkles will disappear.

Doors

If one would take a serious look at things, meaning material items, one that really stands out in my mind is, doors. I know you are thinking, what has doors got to do with a good story?

Well....for one thing, were would we be without them?

Years ago I remember Reg saying to me that the most used doors were on the out-houses and I am inclined to agree with him. As for most parts it was used at the very least around four times a day for each individual.

Laura now she had a different view on the whole thing and said the door that was most used was her pantry door, as us two men folks were always sneaking in there to get something to eat. Not that she condoned it either, just that she wasn't able to keep a steady eye on us two.

For me though, I would have to say the most used doors would be the ones on the barn, as they were being opened and closed hundreds of times a day. First off early in the morning for milking and the feeding of the animals, well....just too many to name actually.

Doors of all kinds too, like the huge sliding one on our barn. Actually there were two. When both were slid opened one could back in a hay wagon with two Clydesdale's and still have room to move

around. One thing I really remember about them huge sliding doors, was Reg and Laura telling me to always make sure they were closed. Reason being that if a storm or high winds would happen by, they could lift the roof right off the barn if left open.

That actually did happen to a friend of ours down the road aways. He had put in the last load of summer hay and went in the house for supper, completely forgetting that he had left the doors open. Later on that night a bad storm happened through and well, the wind got up under the roof and just as nicely as you please, picked it up and set it down in one of his fields. Took him the rest of the summer and most of the fall getting things fixed up.

Today looking back I would say that if there was one thing that was able to bring back memories with a passion, it would be looking at the different types of doors in and around an old farm house or barn.

On our front porch going into the kitchen there was a screen door which was put on for the summer months so the cool summer breezes could blow though our kitchen. Also being a dairy farm we had a good supply of flies which liked to get in every chance they got, but the screen door kept most of them at bay. For the ones it didn't keep out I can still see them long fly strips hanging from our ceiling in the kitchen by the stove. Not heard of today too much, but back then I don't think there was one house or barn without five or six hanging around, maybe more.

Come winter the old screen door would be replaced with a solid wood door to keep the cold east winds from getting at us. Laura didn't like it as she said it closed up the house too much and wasn't healthy. Eventually she managed to get Reg to make her a door with a window in it, sure brightened up the kitchen.

Natural doors are pretty well all gone now, I don't think I have seen one in over sixty years or more. What is a natural door? Well, it was made out of clay mixed with straw. One would make a frame for what ever opening they wanted out of wood. They then would fill it with clay and straw, when done, it would be laid by a huge fire pit to dry and harden. After a day of drying the door could then be used for house, barn or root cellar. Most were used for the root cellars I found, as they were pretty heavy and hard to maneuver. Also being in the root cellar they weren't used as often which allowed them to last longer. Their main purpose was to keep out the cold or heat, which was what one needed in them instances. Ours lasted for the duration and when the root cellar was closed up for good, Reg kept the door putting it in the corner of the barn for a remember when. Often wonder what happened to that old door.

Another door that got my attention, should say two doors was the old double "Z" doors. We had one which led into the horse stall at the

one end of our barn. Reg build the door or doors as at night the team of Clydesdale's seemed to be less restless. Through the day in the winter months when they didn't get out that often the top door would be left open leaving the bottom part closed, but come night and them cold north winds got to blowing they would be both closed up tight. Still can see myself leaning on the bottom of the door talking to them two old Clyde's.

Yes there were many doors that brought back memories. Like walking into the house, *coming in from the barn*, Laura would say as I was hanging up my coat.

"Close the door there boy, were you born in a barn?"

Seems every-time I look at a door my mind gets to wondering what is happening behind them.   Are they hiding a story? I bet they are.

Helpful Hints-Cement For Glass And Iron. Alum melted in an iron spoon over a fire, makes a good cement for joining glass and iron. It is useful for cementing the glass part of a lamp to its metal base and stopping cracks about the base, as paraffin will not penetrate it.

A Place In Time

You know years ago the barn was about the most important building on the farm, other than the house of course. Just the same though, in saying that, I think I spent more time in the barn than I did in the house.

Reason being come 4:00 am we were all up having our morning coffee. Around 4:30 am we were all out in the barn feeding the animals and getting ready for the milking. After milking the pens had to be cleaned and fresh straw put down, and if it happened to be the winter months bales of hay would be broke apart, and a few fork fulls would be given to each critter. I got to say though I sure enjoyed them days and still do today too.

I would have to say that a dairy farm though, is one of a kind when it comes to smells and things. Something like the old General store we used to have in town. Just walking into the place gave me a feeling of warmth, contentment, excitement and happiness. Reason being, well....it was filled with the smells of leather, coffee, sugar, candy and grain, along with the sharp aroma of dill and vinegar that came from the pickle barrels. One might say it was a jumbled mixture of goods, from ladies' hats to saddles, from long handles to crackers.

But the dairy farm has its own special way of broadcasting things to a feller or gal. Like when I walked into our barn, the smells of the saddles and harness's that hung on the wall, was something that made

17

me stop every morning, as if to say, here I am. Once past that, the smell of the hay and straw would seem to just reach out and grab me, letting me know that I am right where I should be at that moment in time. Even today if a good whiff of straw happens by, I'm pitching manure again.

A little further on, old Reg's pipe tobacco makes it's appearance, which tells me exactly where he is working in the barn, never could get enough of that sweet smellin' tobacco. Just before finding Reg, passing the chicken pen is sure a smell that no one could forget, as the ammonia in the air if taken in too fast would almost make you sneeze. But I have to say, if there was ever a smell that was so distinguished, it would be the smell of fresh gathered eggs. I don't know why, just something about them that made me hungry every time I got a whiff of them. Maybe it brought forth the memories of Laura's mornings in the kitchen, cooking, bacon and eggs on the old wood cook stove; I don't know, but I liked it.

The old pig pen now for some folks, was about the most disgusting place in a barn. Not so for our barn though, as we never let it get to the point to where one couldn't stand it. It was my job to keep it clean and fresh straw was put down each and every morning before milking. You know, pigs are one of the cleanest critters in the barn, no kiddin', as they only do their duty in only one end of their pen. The other end is always clean, that is if you keep them supplied with clean bedding.

Now in putting things all into prospective, right here and now, I would have to say my most favorite smells would be the combination of horses, leather, sweat, hay and manure. I don't think there is any better smells in the whole world when all put together.

While saddling up Jennie my horse for an afternoons ride, she would always lay her head on my shoulder and I got to say there isn't anything more beautiful as when I rub my face around her big old nose. Just one thing that a feller or gal would have had to grow up with to appreciate I suppose.

Today, yes the farm has long been put behind me, but in saying that; every time one of them very distinctive smells happens by, it stops me in my tracks, and within seconds I am brought back to a very specific place and moment, a place that everyone I think should visit, at least once throughout a life time.

Helpful Hints-To Remove Fruit Stains. Fruit stains may be removed from table linen by pouring boiling water through the cloth, where it is stained.

Christmas's To Remember

For a lot of years growing up, my Christmas's were something special. Christmas's back then wasn't about buying gifts and things, it was all about being together and enjoying each others company. Today....folks call it an Old-fashioned Christmas.

I sure miss them days, but I will say this, my wife and I still try each and every year to keep a few of them old ways alive.

One way Reg, Laura and my Dad kept us young ones entertained was through stories. Today if a story or two of years gone by comes to mind I am quick to get them down on paper, while the memories are vivid in my mind.

Yes Christmas's was a lot different back then, to start it off a trip back into the bush would be in order. If the snow wasn't too deep the Clyde's would be hooked up to the sleigh and off we would go to find that special tree. If there was too much snow, we would put on our snow shoes, which made things a bit harder, but not one bit less enjoyable.

Usually throughout the summer months our tree would be picked out and we knew exactly where to go to find it. Laura even brought it some fertilizer, *manure* early in the spring, saying it was the least we could do for what it would be giving us come Christmas.

19

The tree would be cut down and either loaded onto the sleigh, or just carried home, with me just busting inside knowing that Santa wasn't too far off.

At home the tree would be stood up and cut to fit where it would be setting. Then it would be brought into the house and put in a pail of sand and given a drink of water mixed with tea and sugar. This Laura said, would keep it well and green for the whole of Christmas, which consisted of at least two weeks.

Ornaments were all hand-made and hung on the tree, along with three store boughten ones from better times. Not that we liked them any better, but it reminded us of the other ways folks decorated their trees.

Every year being the smallest, I would be lifted up so I could put the star on its highest branch, and each and every time something went through me that I couldn't explain. First cold, then warm, what ever it was I looked forward to the sensation to arrive.

The day before Christmas, Laura was busy with cooking. A chocolate cake, two pumpkin pies and one apple would be made all from our garden, or trees near by. Gingerbread cookies were cut out on the table by Laura and I decorated them with raisins, not being allowed to even eat.....just one. Seemed though one or two always got broken through the process though, so I did get my taste.

The neighbor up the road always dropped by with a bag of walnuts from his black walnut tree and Laura always rewarded him with a glass or two of her home made punch. The walnuts would be opened and the insides would be spread on her muffins she would make and I gotta' tell ya, they were delicious. Could never figure though, what was in that punch, as it never ceased to amaze me how red old Jessie's face got after just two cups. I will say this, he never missed a Christmas in all the years that I've known him.

Christmas Eve arrived and supper was set on the table. *My mouth still waters thinking about Laura's cooking.* After supper Reg and myself went to the barn, he bedded down the critters while I rubbed down Jennie my horse, which rewarded me with a hug, as she swung her big old neck around mine. A bucket ot oats would be given with a few kind words, then off we would go back to the house.

Once inside we all gathered around the old cook stove and Laura would lite the kerosene lamp and bring out some goodies. Once settled, Reg would get to tellin' some of his tales from years past or ones that he had heard, that he felt deserved a second hearing. I have to tell you, if there was a time in my life that I never wanted to end, it was then. But with all good things an end is always somewhere in the future and for me on this night it was bed. Before heading up stairs

though, my stocking was hung by the Christmas tree, along with a few cookies and a glass of milk for Santa.

Christmas morning, Laura was up before the sun and a big goose would be put in the oven.

While eating breakfast my eyes never left the tree, as below it lied one special gift for me. Nothing compared to what folks get today, but to me....it was a treasure that was just waiting to be found. If and when gifts were given, they mostly were homemade, but occasionally some silk would be bought for Laura as she loved it so.

Presents were opened and I think if we would have had neighbors close by they would have thought we were in trouble with all the cheers.

Once things settled and our gifts had been opened the chores had to be done. Later on friends dropped by and the chatting just never seemed to stop until supper time.

The table would then be covered with Laura's favorite red checkered table cloth, then set with her best dishes and silverware, that only came out on special occasions. Not that they cost a lot, as they didn't, but they were just a few items that Laura kept for days like this. She would say. "It's a womans thing George, just enjoy them."

I wasn't one to argue either, not with all them goodies sittin' around just waiting for me to try.

Christmas supper was special to say the least, but not one bit would be taken before grace was said, not on this day. Once said, the goose was taken out of the oven, and the smell alone got everyone in the rooms mouth to drooling, especially mine.

While eating, laughter could be heard, and stories were told. I have to say the thing I enjoyed the most was listening to the stories, but watching the faces of the folks as they listened was sure something special to see in itself. Might say they were burned into my mind, never to be lost.

We might have been poor money wise back then, but we sure were wealthy with what really matters. Merry Christmas folks.

Helpful Hints-To Remove Soot. Should soot fall upon the carpet, cover it with dry salt and it may be swept up without leaving smears.

Elders

You know throughout my life I have seen a lot of things change, some for the good but some for the bad too. It sure saddens me to see the way things are going, especially with our elders. The weathered faces of some show the hardships that they have endured throughout their everyday lives. Life wasn't easy for them that's for sure and if you listen to some of their stories you will never hear any words relating to feeling sorry for themselves. That's pretty amazing in itself, just think about it in today's world with all the complaints and things being thrown around from person to person.

Years ago folks had hard times but they didn't go out and look for others to fix their problems, they handled the problems all on their own. For that matter if you weren't real close to them you would never know that they had problems, as it was not the thing to do in letting others know that you were having a bad day.

It was looking down on someone if you were to give them hand outs, not that they were readily available. One didn't take charity in other words, it was an insult to their good nature. If one wanted to do something to help out, they might all come

together on haying time for example. The women would all get together and bake the meals and the men folks would all get together and bring in the hay. They would be at one farm one day another the next and so on till it was all done up for the winter. That wasn't charity, that was just helping each other and using ones mind in a way that saved each other a pile of hard work.

Our elders are slowly becoming a thing of the past as everyone can see. The thing is, which bothers me some, is so much will be lost when they are gone and no one right now seems to be too worried about that. The knowledge and wisdom that a lot of these elders have could save and help the new generation for years to come; if one just started talking to the older folks and writing things down and most importantly using some of the advice in their every day lives. I know for myself I have talked to and been raised by older folks and every word that they have told me has ended up helping me throughout my life. Sure there is a bit of humor there, even a bit of made up things, but even with that there is something to be learned if one just takes the time to listen.

I hear today of some of the schools going in and singing to the older folks and telling them about their day, that's all good and fine, but maybe we should be going in once a week and letting the elders tell the younger ones a bit of their past life and in doing so I am sure the young ones would leave with a lot more than what they had when they came in.

Another way would be for those that have family that are getting a bit older to sit down and get them to talking about their days of years ago, but don't just listen, write things down. Reason being our minds just don't have enough room in todays world to take it all in and remember it. If it's wrote down, one will have it to look back on in times of need.

Times are changing fast today and if we don't take the time to talk to our elders we will have lost so much. I know a lot of folks of today want to do things their way and that's fine, but the things that folks want to do might not be good enough if our old world falls into hard times. If that should happen, I would guess that many would just perish, as they would not know how to look after themselves. Today the powers that be has everyone depending on them and this was not a mistake.

Remember, it's only my opinion, but with saying that, every now and then opinions are worth while reading or listening to.

So the next time you see an old feller or gal sitting on a bench or rocking chair, why not drop by and say hello, you never know, you might learn something, new or....old....or Hmm....

Helpful Hints-To Dry Woolens Without Shrinking. An old time woolen manufacturer at one time said. That woolen garments should be hung on the line dripping wet and not wrung out at all. If done this way the shrinkage will be almost unnoticeable.

Education

You know the values in life, is what makes one realize how much your life is really worth. For me I didn't get too much education, well at least not from the big fancy schools of today. My education came from an old one room school house. One teacher, eight grades and the one teacher taught us all.

Never ceases to amaze me how this lady had time for each and every one of us. At that time thinking back, she had about fifty or sixty young ones to tend to and never neglected a one. Over the years she not only taught me reading, writing and arithmetic, but she taught me to listen to my elders, as she knew that their wisdom was what we would use most in our every day life. So for me I took her words of wisdom to heart and I listened to my elders and still do today, even though I am in that elder age bracket now myself. My circle of old friends is getting smaller, but what I do is try and make new friends. Ones that think along the same line as I do, that way we can get to some serious chattin' now and again.

But getting back to my education, I went through all eight grades in that one room school house, not only learning but also a lot of good memories were made too.

Life changes though, and my Dad came to take me back home from the place I was boarded out at. I was sad and happy at the same time. Sad to leave Reg, Laura and Grey Wolf, but happy to be with my old Dad again. Not sure now, that if I would have known what laid ahead,

what I would have done. But at the time I was still young and my real Dad was where I decided I needed to be.

Once back on his farm I was introduced to a new school, it was much bigger, had a room for each grade and a separate teacher for each grade. I remember distinctly the first day I arrived on the new schools door step. A teacher took me in and sat me down for a chat. I told her I had gone through public school and this visit was just to set things straight, that I should not really be here, I should be in my first year of high school. The teacher was really nice, but she wasn't listening. She then tried to explain that children that comes from country schools, such as I went to are usually two years behind and that I would have to be dropped back two years.

I was really upset and fit to be tied, I couldn't see myself sitting in a room filled with children younger than me, knowing that I was from the country. They would just make my life miserable. Kids can be cruel and I was a kid, so I knew.

Well I got up and left with her running behind me.

"You have to stay here and talk to the principal George, you can't just up and leave."

"You just watch me," I said, and out the door I went. I took my time but headed on home to tell my Dad what had happened and what they had told me.

When I got home and told dad he was madder than a bull that just got stung on the behind by a hornet. Down to the school we went, in the front door and passed right by a dozen teachers and right into the principals office. One teacher tried to stop us, but it just wasn't going to happen. Inside Dad pulled up two chairs and told me to sit down.

You have to understand, my Dad was a huge man and when someone said something against country folks or his family, well that made his blood boil.

He then sat down himself and got to telling the principal what he thought.

"First thing here Mr. Principal, my son here went though all eight grades. He is as smart as any other kid in your so called school and he will be going to high school and further more; George here has had not only the teaching of an excellent teacher, he has the upbringing of two loving and smart farmers, along with an Indian friend named, Grey Wolf. I would say he probably knows as much about life as we both do."

The principal then sat back and said. "We do have a test he could take that would settle all this and I would like to talk to him alone."

"OK," said Dad, "lets get at it."

Dad told me to do what they asked and said he would be right outside.

26

The test I took, along with a long talk with the principal; Dad was called back in and nothing more was said. I was given my papers and was off to high school. He told Dad later that in reality, I should be in grade ten, not nine and maybe even higher.

So there you have it, a bit about my education and how us country boys had to fight for our rights in a growing world.

Helpful Hints-To Get Rid Of Flies. It is said you will not be troubled with flies if you keep geraniums growing in the house. Then why not have more flowers and fewer flies.

Cookies

Cookies, now there is something any young feller, or for that matter, this old feller, can't get enough of.

I have to say back on the farm Laura used to make the best cookies one could ever wish for. Now don't get me wrong later on in life I have come upon a few women that made some pretty good ones too. Like my wife, I would have to say she has a way about her when it comes to making cookies, just as Laura did. Not just saying that because she is my wife either. If you want proof just drop by some day when she is making them, I'd gladly let you have one to try.

I can remember on them cold winter days coming in from the fields, smelling them cookies as I got closer to the house. Sure made a young feller feel good about coming home. Cookies are something in my eyes that have to be made not so thick, that you just want one. They need to be thin enough so you can eat about six, as having six on a plate, sure looked like you had something.

There is only one thing better than cookies on a plate and that was cookies on a plate and a hot chocolate to back them up with. Thing is, that hot chocolate back in them days was sure made differently than today. Back then folks used fresh raw cream right from their cows, or neighbors cows and no matter how one tries in todays world, it just can't be matched. I still enjoy a hot chocolate today with cookies but

once you had the taste of real cream, well, I always finished up feeling like I was missing something.

Cookie making is almost a thing of the past now a days, as folks figure they can buy them in store so cheap it isn't worth their while or time making them. Thing is they are wrong. As my wife will tell you that they are easily made, not forgetting to mention how much healthier they are for you.

I have bought a few in my days I will say that, but when it comes time to eat one I find one is enough and the rest get thrown out. Just can't get myself to liking them store bought ones no matter how hard I try. For one thing, have you ever read what goes into them, in the ingredient section on the package? Sheesh! some of the things I can't even pronounce and I went all the way through public school. On that subject, I figure it this way, if I can't pronounce the words of what is in the cookie, I sure as heck should not be eating it.

What made me bring a story to life about cookies? Well, just so happens my wife was making them while I was here working on a column of mine. What kind of cookies you ask? Molasses cookies, they are one of my most favorites, along with sugar cookies, double layer with some fresh fruit in the middle and to top it off, a coat of vanilla icing on top. Boy, I might not be a young feller in body any more, but when it comes to my lovely wife's cookies, I sure am in mind.

Certain things throughout my life have stayed with me, taking me back to a time when things were not without hardships, but a time that when a simple thing like a cookie could make a young fellers day take on a whole new meaning.

Now, if your real good, I will just go and get myself a couple of them cookies and enjoy one with you.

Helpful Hints-To Make Hard Water Soft. Fill your pot with hard water and set on stove. Then put half a cup of wood ashes into a woolen bag covered with a cotton cloth to prevent the sifting out of the ashes and hang the bag in the water till the water is warm. You now have soft water.

Farm Critters

By the lane-way each morning, throughout summer, I would swing the huge steel gate open to let the cows head off to the pasture for feeding. Through the winter months they pretty well stayed in the barn where it was warm, only going out on nice days and staying close to the barn. Seems they knew where their food for the day was coming from. Lot of folks figure animals are not too smart, but I beg to differ.

For example, pigs, they love to dig in mud holes, get all dirty and have a good old time but inside their pen it's a different story. As I have said in other stories, the trick is that the inside of their pen has to be kept clean. If you give them fresh straw every day, they will take one end of the pen and make it into a nice place to lay and that spot will be kept that way. In our barn at any given time through the winter months, you could come in and you would have to search for the pigs, as they would be buried down under the straw. Seems they just loved it under there enjoying the warmth and each others company. At the other end of the pen that's where they do their duty. I have always admired them in how organized they keep things. Reg used to say, "better than some....I know." Of course, if I didn't keep the pen clean and just let it go, well then you would have some dirty pigs.

Horses now are also a clean animal and just love fresh strawed quarters. I had a pen in one end of our barn, where the two Clyde's and Jennie my riding horse was kept. They mingled and I swear they would talk to each other, as they were always together and when I

came into the barn they would look at each other giving me a funny look. Especially the two Clyde's, they were sole mates for life them two, as no matter what they did through their life they did it together, right up till their end. Still makes me sad when I think of their ending, so....won't go there.

The cows now, they are a different sort of critter for sure. They don't mind getting dirty, but will stay relatively clean if a fellow keeps their stall clean, which we did. Each cow had their own stall, all in a row in the barn. At one end was a trough where I fed them, usually just before milking as it kept them busy and not buggin' me.

The thing I remember and miss the most about them days, was in the evening hours. Laura would come out to the barn from her kitchen, usually wearing her apron and a long dress. I would open the large gate, which led to the pasture where the cows were feeding. Laura then would put her hands to her mouth and call, "Here Co', boss! co', boss! co'! co'! Co'!" "Here Co', boss! co', boss! co'! co'! co'!" and then we would wait. A few minutes later here would come the cows, along with a couple young calves walking all in a row, headin' to the barn. I would open the barn door and each and every one would go to her own stall. They just knew when Laura called them, it was feeding and milking time.

The only problems we would have was when we had a young one once in awhile that wouldn't come when called. That's where our small collie dog came into the picture. Laura would then say, "go get that stubborn critter collie dog," and off she would go. A few more minutes would pass and down the lane-way it would come, just a running with the collie nipping at it heals and it calling for its mother. The collie didn't hurt it by no means, but by nipping at their heels it sure got their attention and moving in the right direction. Yep those were the days.

I can also still visualize Laura standing there with her arm around my shoulders as the cows passed us by and once in, she would kneel down and give me a big old hug. She would then say. "How about you and me going and getting a nice hot chocolate and a couple of them just baked cookies before milking?"

In we would go and I would take up my position in the wood-box, waiting for the cook stove to warm up the milk for chocolate and usually the rocking chair was pulled close to the warmth of the stove and Laura would share a story or two of her younger days, and the day moved forward.

Helpful Hints-To Remove Mildew. Dip article into sour buttermilk, lay in the sun to whiten and wash in clean water.

Farming

You know years ago things on the old farm were done a lot different than today. One example would be that the family farm was handed down from generation to generation. Thing that most folks don't realize is that farming isn't something that can be taught in schools. Oh sure they tell ya that it can be but it can't. They can show you the basics, let you look at pictures and given the benefit of doubt, maybe tell you how many gallons of pesticides one has to use per acre. There is other things too that one will be shown, but what I mentioned should give you an idea of what my meaning is.

What happens is, that a fellow or gal is born right into farm life. In the beginning he watches his Dad and Mom as they go about their daily chores and learns. When they get older they then are all ready for hands on, and their fathers and mothers take them into the fields and teach them things, like smell, how soil should look, how to plant crops, what to do when one has a drought and how to deal with it. Then there is the knowledge one learns in how to overcome hardships, dealing with governments, law practices, stores, implement dealers, just too many to name as the list goes on.

Then one has to learn how to repair his own equipment and learn how to operate them. You can't learn how to drive a tractor pulling a plow in school. You can't trim a pear or apple tree there either. Lots of things like that come into play. The only way one learns these things is if he is raised on a farm or born into a family of farmers. Simple as that.

Problem today is that the powers that be want you to be dependant on them, which is the wrong way to living a good healthy prosperous life. I have found that if I wanted to go ahead in this world I had to be self efficient, relying on no one. Well maybe no one other than my lovely wife. As they say, behind every successful farmer is a good wife.

Another thing I had to use was my own judgment when it came to doing things, along with every so often doing what I feel is right in my gut.

Farming isn't an easy life either; some folks aren't cut out for it. There are long hours, like from day light to dark. Even when one gets to their beds at nights, they still usually lay there for an hour or two just thrashing out what had happened through their day. Then once that is set in their mind, they get to thinking about the next days work and how they are going to handle it.

So why is it that our farms are slowly disappearing, some will say.

"It's just too hard of a life. Can't make a living off the land any more."

Well some parts of them answers are correct, as farming is a hard life, and yes it is hard to make a living off the land today. But why? Well, I will tell you why. The reason folks can't make a living off the land is that, that is all they really want to do. They want to make money. Some say, well what the heck is wrong with that? I say well if your going to get into farming for just money, well that's your first biggest mistake. Like myself, farming was handed down to me. I knew the way of going about it the day I was born. I guess you could say it was in my blood. But the biggest thing is just what I said. If money is all that is getting you into the farming business, well let me just say right here and now, forget it.

Farming is something that you have to love to do, you have to feel it in your heart. My old Dad and myself loved to get up every morning and get out to the fields, couldn't wait till breakfast was over to get our hands into some good old dirt.

Today though our farms are almost extinct you might say and what a shame. Our lands have been covered up with pavement and cement. Prime land has been sold for industries. The powers that be then got into it and put so darn many rules and regulations into effect, that it choked the life right out of the old fellers. Places that sold our produce was taken away from us bringing in free trade from other countries. Once the imports started to flow in, all our canning factories and wineries started to close their doors.

So....too late now most folks say. Just have to put it behind us and let other countries take care of us. Well through my eyes they are wrong in that way of thinking.

What could and should be done is for the small farmers to try and make a come back. The younger folks of today should be seeking out the elders of years past and start asking questions and doing it fast as their isn't too many of us still kickin'. They should then buy up a small piece of land and get to growing some things. Not for money, but to grow enough just for themselves and their family.

Once you are into it a few extra dollars will be following close behind. Remember this, big is not the way to go. I know they tell you that it is, but the folks that have that thinking on their minds are only in it for money. That's why they have failed and that is why they will keep on failing. I should say here that going big all the time just doesn't mean farming it can be any type of business.

Well I guess I have said my piece, but remember this, if you really like working with soil, growing your own and just have a love like nothing else for 'Mother Nature', well then maybe, just maybe, farming might be for you. Good luck.

Helpful Hints-Weights And Measures. One pound of butter is equal to a pint. Ten eggs are equal to a pound. A pound of brown or white sugar equals a pint. A pound and two ounces of either wheat flour or corn meal is equal to a quart. Eight large tablespoonfuls are equal to a gill, or in todays world, a half a cup. Thirty two large tablespoonfuls equal a pint. A common size wine-glass, holds four tablespoons, or half a cup. Four ordinary tea cups of liquid equal one quart.

Helpful Hints-To Loosen Covers Of Fruit Jars. Place the cover in hot water for two or three minutes and they may be easily unscrewed.

Finer Things In Life

For most folks having a drink of water is as simple as walking over to a tap, turning it and running off a glass or two. For myself though it wasn't quite that easy. If asked though which water I liked the best, it would be well water other than city water.

Main reason would be that good well water isn't full of man made chemicals that in my mind, simply put, makes one sick over time.

Many a day I remember my Dad and myself coming in from the fields sweaty and hot from a days work, both walking right up to the old hand pump on the well. Usually there was a pail with water sittin' beside it that we used to prime it with to get it flowing. Never had a pump that held its prime.

I would usually pump for Dad first as he bend down and put his head under the water. He then would take off his hat fill it half full of cool water and swish it around and dump it on the ground. Once done it would be set back on his head and out would come his old handkerchief which he would use to dry himself off a touch. Most though would be left for the air of summer to take care of.

Once he was finished it would be my turn and I did pretty well the same as he had done, might say it made me feel like a man to do things like my old Dad.

After we both got cleaned up and looked half respectable it was time for a nice cool drink. Any water that had been laying in the pump itself, or from the priming of the pump was now well washed clean.

The cup we had back then was made out of tin which hung on a nail on a tree which grew beside the well. We would then sit back on a couple crates which Dad had kickin' around and slowly sip at the cool fresh water. After only two cups the thirst just seemed to vanish leaving you with a contentment which is hard to explain. We would then sit there enjoying what was left of the day and then head on into the house for supper.

For a number of years our water for the house was taken from the well and carried into the house for drinking, washing and cooking. A pail of fresh water would set on a stool by the door going out onto the porch, with a cup hooked to its side. Anyone happening by that wanted a drink would just dip the cup into the pail and drink away, hanging it back up for the next person. If the pail was about empty, who ever was the last to have a drink would go out and filler' up. In all my years I never ever heard one person complain about having to go and get it.

Today folks would say that was unsanitary as one could get sick drinking from a cup that someone else has drank from, but I never seen it happen in our home. My way of looking at it is that today folks are protected too much and their bodies have lost all the immunities to fight off disease.

Later on we eventually bought a pump for our counter in the kitchen which sure was nice come winter, as we didn't have to go out in the cold to bring it in anymore. We did have a few problems at first with the line freezing up, but eventually we got it fixed with burying it a bit deeper from the well to the house and wrapping the part where it came out of the ground up and into the house with insulation.

You know in the very beginning we didn't even have steel pails for water or for milking, as they were made out of wood, same as barrels for that matter. Wood in my mind is a lot better than steel as they seemed to outlast any steel one I ever owned. The only thing one would have to do with the wood ones would be to keep them damp now and then so they kept swollen up, which kept the joints nice and tight so they didn't leak.

Actually our horse troughs were made out of wood and in all the years I lived on the farm I never seen one leak a drop, or heard any horse complain for that matter.

And finally a great saying my old Grandfather used to say each and every time he had a drink from our well.

"You know George, one never realizes what water is worth, till the well is dry, so enjoy it while you can."

First Visit To The Doc

Every now and then, reflecting back to my younger days, I get to thinking of my first visit to the doctors office, it wasn't by my choosing either.

Fall had come early and most of the leaves were off the trees. I had been helping Reg bring in logs to cut up for firewood and was about to head on in for supper. All the logs were laying in a pile and the reins for the team of horses was laying on the top of a few. I climbed up to get them and I guess with the logs being so wet and slippery I went for a tumble. I came down on my wrist scraping it as I fell. I still can remember the pain and I knew I messed things up. Reg came over and had a look and in the house we went. Laura washed the cut and put some ointment on it and then wrapped it up. I was then told to go lay down by the fire and try and relax for a bit. Sure was hard to do as the pain just seemed to shoot though my whole arm.

Well eventually the pain eased off, but by morning the cut started to swell up. Laura looked at it and went and got Reg. I don't like the look of this cut here and think you had better take him to see old Doc Jones. I sure didn't want to go, as anything I ever heard about doctors, well, wasn't good. At any rate, being so young I didn't have any say in the matter.

A few minutes later, Reg got the old truck out from its bed and we headed on into see the Doc. It was a few miles away as we didn't have one in our town and had to go to a neighboring town. Reg he wasn't

too much for talking, so my mind was left to think all kinds of things. What was going to happen when I got there, was he going to put that red ointment they called Iodine on it, man I sure hope not, that stuff was worse than the cut itself. Brought tears to my eyes when they used that.

Well we finally got there and in we went. I remember it like it was happening today. The old Doc had a lady for a nurse and she came right over. She could tell I had hurt my hand as it being bandaged up and all. She took my hand and said, "oh my it is sure swollen up isn't it and I bet it hurts like the dickens?"

"It sure does," I said, and with that she led us to another room where the doctor was.

He was sitting behind an old desk and when he saw me he got up and came over to my side.

"Well looks like you got yourself a bit of a problem here young fellow."

"Yep, afraid so I said."

"Well sit down here and let me have a look at it." That I did and he took off the cloth that Laura had wrapped it with.

"Sure is swollen he said, for sure got some infection in it, but not to worry, I will clean it up."

With that I spoke up, "not that red stuff doc, not that red stuff?"

He looked down at me and said, "George is it?"

"Yep," I said.

"Well George, I don't use that kind anymore, we have a new kind. Does the same job and for most parts even better."
I gave a sigh of relief!

He then asked the nurse to get some cleaning solution and bring it to him. While she was gone, he got to asking me all kinds of questions, like how it happened, which way I fell, just too many to name here. He then went to the fridge which he had in his office and took out a soda.

"Would you like one?" he asked.

"Would I, I said, I would love one." With that he handed it to me and an opener.

"Can you manage?" he said.

"Sure, no problem and eased my sore hand into position to open it."

"Hmm he said, you just solved one of my thoughts, your hand is not broken. If it was you wouldn't be opening that pop the way you did." I never thought a thing about it, as I didn't get to drinkin' soda very often and this was a real treat.

Well he cleaned me up, gave me some medicine and we were on our way. I thanked him for the soda and not using the red stuff and out to the truck we went.

Over the years I went to old doc Jones a few times and he got to know me real good and me him. Doctors back then had a way of doing things, they didn't have all the fancy equipment they have today and hardly ever sent anyone in for x-rays and things. They took time with you and they learned all about their patient and when anything went wrong they were on top of it and new pretty well what any problem was.

I know today they say we are short of doctors for the amount of people we have. But if you think back to my early days, there might have only been one doctor for hundreds of miles and he managed to look after everyone.

In my books today, the powers that be, should be recruiting more doctors, in other words training our own, right here in Canada. Some say the folks here don't want to learn, so they have to go to other countries. I say there is plenty of folks here that would love to learn the trade in helping others, just that it is too hard and too expensive for them to go about it. We need to be putting things in place that will make it tempting to the new students, or in other words give them the incentive that is needed.

Like an old mule I once had. That old son of a gun every once in awhile wouldn't move, just stopped in its track. Only way I could get it going again was to dangle a carrot in front of its nose. Get my meaning? If that was done, within a few years we would have all the doctors we need.

Since moving here to Port Loring its been hard for me and my wife to find a full time family doctor, especially one I can sit and talk to for a bit, one that will listen to me, one like old Doc Jones. I suppose them days are gone, but if one happens by, or one happens upon this story, give me a call. I sure would like to hear from you.

I did get to know a doctor here not too far away from our home, whom actually wrote a poem for my last book, Dr. Wood, great man. Only problem there is, that he only comes to our town once a month and for most parts unless you are pretty ill you don't get to see him. You now are sent in other directions. Too bad too, as he is one of them fellers that you can really feel comfortable with, like old Doc Jones. I should also say that he is still there for me.

Helpful Hints-Treatment For New Iron Pots. Iron pots should be boiled out with wood ashes and cold water, then thoroughly washed. They are then ready to use.

Greasy iron pots are best cleaned while hot. An addition of a little soda to the first water will make them more easy to clean.

Fishing

It was a beauty of a spring day, the sun was shinning through my bedroom window searching for my eyes to tell me it was time I got up. Living on the dairy farm we hardly ever got to sleep in late, but on this morning I was left alone to wake on my own.

Being the 24th of May I decided it would be a good day for fishing. I climbed out of bed, got dressed and headed on down stairs. I was greeted with the smell of fresh ham and eggs cooking on the old wood stove. I gotta' say, one of my most favorite times, was breakfast sittin' on the table come morning, as the smells would just fill the house. I swear, my old stomach would growl so loud that you could hear it outside if you happened to be listening.

"Sit down at the table there George," Laura would say. "Breakfast is just about ready." I could sit there for hours watching her cooking away and once in awhile like this morning, she would get to humming.

Amazing Grace was her most favorite tune, I wasn't sure what it was all about at the time, but it sure was soothing to the ears. I could listen to it all day.

As the first plate hit the table, Reg walked in from outside. He had been out finishing up the milking at the barn and you could tell he was hungrier than a bear. He took his old pipe out of his mouth, knocked it clean into the stove and put it away in his pipe box which hung on a nail on the wall by the door. He was never without a pipe in his mouth, other than when he was eating.

He got washed up, sat down at the table and poured himself a cup of fresh perked coffee.

"Nice day out there," he said, "any plans for this fine day George?"

"Well I had planned on going fishing if it is OK with you?"

"OK with me." he said, "as long as you get your chores done up as soon as you get home."

"Yep will do," I said, "one thing though Reg, I don't have a pole, would you have one I could borrow?"

"Borrow? Heck can't have that, young feller needs a fishing pole, after breakfast we will head on out to the willow tree and cut you one. I even got some spare line kickin' around here somewhere."

We then got to eating and for a short time nothing was said. Not that we didn't have anything to talk about, just that we didn't want to take anything away from Laura's cookin'. And besides, there wasn't a minute that our mouths weren't full.

Once done we headed on out to the tree and Reg reached up and picked a real nice branch.

"Here is a good one," he said and brought it down so we could cut it. With that he then took out his jack knife and me with mine we both went to work and skinned it. Reg then took some line and attached it to the end of the pole wrapping the remaining line around the pole, then putting on a hook he had made out of an old piece of barb wire fence. Once that was done he went into the house and brought out an old cork he saved from an old bottle and slit a small hole through it and tied it on the line about two feet above the hook.

"Well," he said, "looks like you are all set to go fishing."

"Looks that way, just got to get a few worms."

"Well you go get your worms, but I got something that the fish likes even better."

"Really?" I asked, "What would that be?"

"Well, Laura cooked fresh ham this morning and I have to tell ya, fish likes nothing better than fresh ham. Most folks would never think of them liking it, but they sure do, you try it and let me know how you make out when you get home."

"I sure will," I said and I was off. I did dig up a few worms for a back up, but it wasn't necessary as I was to find out.

For years I used that old pole, not like the equipment they got today I know, but one thing was for sure, it got the job done, as I caught more fish with it than I could begin to count.

Oh and that ham for bait, well......I have to tell you, that cork that Reg gave me for a bobber, well it never seen the light of day, as I was too busy pullin' them in.

Things were simpler back then I will say that, but what more could a fellow ask for?

Full Moons

You know thinking back to my younger days, we had quite a different outlook on things. In actuality there was probably a lot of things that we did that some have never even heard of.

Take the full moons of the year. Back then we looked at each full moon as something special, not just as an object in the sky. So that got me to thinking, and...thought I would share a bit about each month of the year and what the full moon meant to us, many years ago.

My best friend Grey Wolf called January's moon the Wolf Moon, as the wolves years ago would howl around the camp fires at night. He looked forward to that month more than any other month of the year.

But for Reg, Laura and myself, we called it the Beginning moon as it was the start of a whole new year. I can still remember standing in front of my window at night wishing upon it, for things that I wanted most in life. I should mention that a lot came true.

Grey Wolf called February's moon, the Snow moon, as that was when the heaviest snow used to fall, and Laura and Reg too. Some though called it the Cold moon like me, as that was the month I hated the most, especially when visiting the old out-house in the middle of the night.

Grey Wolf called March's moon the Worm moon, as that was when the soil started to thaw out and things started to warm up a bit. To the settlers in the early days it was called the Lenten moon, as it was the

last full moon of winter. But for me, I called it, the Maple Tree moon as that is when the syrup started to flow, and I can still see Laura, Reg and myself headin' off back to the sugar bush. Sure miss them days.

Grey Wolf called April's moon the Pink moon as that was when the flowers, like the wild ground Phlox started to bloom, which was pink in color for most varieties. For Reg, Laura and myself though, we got to callin' it the Birthday moon. Reason being, April was the month my birthday fell on. Always looked forward to that month, still do. Home made chocolate cake time.

Grey Wolf called May's moon the Flower moon as that was when most of the wild flowers started to bloom. Laura and Reg along with myself called it the Milk moon as around that time of year the cows started giving a larger amount of milk, and so....good tasting. Gotta' say, I sure miss that fresh raw milk.

Grey Wolf called June's moon, the Sweet moon as that was when the wild strawberries made an appearance. Some Natives called it the Strawberry moon. For me I called it the Eating moon, as when Laura picked and brought in them berries for the first time, I couldn't wait to cover them with fresh cream from the mornings milking, and well, you know the rest. Any way you look at it though, it was a Strawberry moon.

Grey Wolf called July's moon the Buck moon, as that was the month when the antlers start to form on the buck deers. For Reg, Laura and mostly me, we called it the Storm moon, as that was the month we got the real bad thunder and lightning storms. Still see myself laying there at night watching the light from the lightning flash through my bedroom window.

Grey Wolf called August's moon the Fishing moon, as that was when he did most of his fishing. One of his most favorite times thinking back. For me it was the Hot moon, as that was the month that I laid awake the most, waiting for a cool breeze to come through my bedroom window so that I could fall asleep.

Grey Wolf called September's moon the Corn moon, as he said he still could remember his mother picking the corn for his evening meals. For me it was called the Back to School moon. Not one of my most favorites, at least not back then. Did have some good times in school though.

Grey Wolf called October's moon the South moon, as that was when he would say his goodbyes to me and head off to the warmer climate. For Reg, Laura and myself it was called the Harvest moon as many other farmers. As that was when most all our crops were ready for harvesting. Great month no matter what way you look at it.

Grey Wolf called November's moon the Beaver moon, as he said he still can remember his father and mother setting traps for the warm

furs that would surely be needed. For me I called it the Sad moon, as things were put away for winter, my horse Jennie was not being rode as much due to slippery weather, and most days were spent either in the barn, or the house trying to keep warm. Good life though just the same.

And finally, December, Grey Wolf called December's moon, the Long cold moon, as that was the start of winter in his eyes, as many cold days will follow. For me, well you all know what I called that one, don't ya? Yep your right, I called it the Christmas moon, and the only thing on my mind that month was Santa Clause. Simple as that.

So there you go a few different ways of how Grey Wolf, Reg, Laura and myself felt every night, when we looked up into that big old night sky. It was a good time to be alive.

Still is, lookin' up with my lovely wife by my side.

Helpful Hints-The Teakettle. In localities where there is lime in the water, it is well to keep egg shells in the teakettle to receive the lime deposits.

Got The Time

Y ou know for most folks, telling time is a pretty simple thing. Now a days one usually has at the least, three or four clocks on the wall. In our house today we have one wined up wall clock that was given to us by a real nice lady from Germany. Just wined it up and it usually lasts for about three or four weeks. Nice to have in case the power goes out, but then again there is a lot of battery operated clocks too. We have one of them but it never keeps good time, always around ten minutes slow or fast. Not too sure why we even keep it, I suppose we are just sentimental as we have had it for so many years and hate to throw it out, might say it's part of the family.

We also have one in the bedroom that plugs into the wall and it's pretty accurate, just that around our area here in Port Loring we have a lot of power surges and only takes a second and out it goes, then has to be set again. At least once a week I get to hear my wife saying a few choice words while resetting it.

For years now I have carried an old pocket watch that you wound up and it works quite well, as long as you don't forget to wined it, only thing is I put it down somewhere the other day and now can't find the darn thing. Old mind is the first thing to go I suppose, or some say.

My boys, Craig and Karl bought me a new pocket watch a few years ago and I have been saving it for a special occasion, so being I can't find my other one I figured I would give it a try. Problem I got now is, I guess it runs on a small battery and since I haven't used it for two years the battery is dead in it. So got the wife to put it in her purse so I know where it is and when we go to town will get it fixed up.

I don't know why really that I enjoy carrying a watch, just one of those things. One watch I could never wear though was one that slips onto your wrist. Just don't seem practical to me and also when I was on the farm I seen so many folks getting it hooked up on things. One fellow was climbing up the side of my truck while helping me unload one time at the Farmers Market. He some how got it hooked up on the top rack of the truck and slipped, well the watch almost tore his hand right off. That kind of clinched it for me, decided after that I would much sooner have the old watch in my pocket or vest pocket.

Going way back though in my younger days I never had a watch, but then I never worried about time. One just went to the fields or barn to work and when he or she was done you came home. Old Dad though did teach me a way of telling time while out in the fields and it was really quite simple. On our farm all our rows of fruit and grapes were always planted from north to south. Nice thing about that, I was taught to just look at my shadow and standing north to south you could pretty well tell what time it was by just looking at it. Noon was easy or just before or after, as your shadow would be straight in front of you. I bet we were never late for dinner in all them years we farmed.

Don't really need the rows of fruit or grapes to tell a fellow though, as long as you know where north is you can get the time of day any time you want it. Oh and as long as the sun is shinning, pretty hard to tell time if you don't have a shadow.

Out back of our house I picked up a couple old sundials one time and set them on a rock and its kind of neat having them there. No special reason, just that every time I go by them it gives me a good feeling knowing that it is just one more way of getting by without all those high tech gadgets. I should also say that you can also tell time by just looking at the sun, as if it is right overhead, it's about lunch time. Many times I remember my old Dad looking up at the sun, wiping the sweat off his brow and saying.

"Well George, dinner time, what you say we go eat."

So there you have it, a bit on how some of us old timers told time years ago and for that matter still do today.

Helpful Hints-Icy Windows. Rub the windows with a sponge dipped in alcohol and the windows will be kept free of ice. Alcohol is also good to polish them with. No smoking when up close to glass.

Grey Wolf & Wisdom

"**Y**ou know young one, we have become good friends over the years and my thoughts have been on that question you asked me, when I first met you."

"There has been a lot of questions that I have asked, that you have not answered Grey Wolf. I didn't push the matter as I figured you had reasons."

"Reasons were that you were not ready for the answers young one. I told you what you needed to know at the time. But on the matter of the first question which was, why I lived alone in this small cottage away from most humans?"

"Now I remember."

"Do you know how you came to being here in this country young one?"

"Well, not really, I guess I was just born here and things happened and here I am."

"Well there is much more to it than that. It would take years for me to share all the knowledge that you will be needing, but for now I shall share some. In the beginning there was no white man living amongst us. We lived a simple, happy life. We were in the millions strong, with over a thousand different tribes located in what you call the United States today.

When the white folks came, also came diseases that made our people very sick, thousands died. Eventually our people were herded

47

like cattle into locations they called reservations. They took away our lifestyle and promoted their own. It was not a good time, young one."

"Gee Grey Wolf, us white folks did all that?"

"That and much more. It saddens me to think back on what has happened, remembering all that we had, and all that has been lost. Some things though will be never lost. Like my wanting to live alone with nature, listening and learning from what each day brings to me. You know, my people enjoy their privacy as much as you do in your home, just that we choose to go about things different than you do. I know some white folks think we should change to their ways and some of our people have. I believe our world as what once was is changing so fast, that if something isn't done soon we might loose everything.

I also believe that the Great Spirit is saddened by what he sees, but I also think through his wisdom, along with our Grandfathers and Grandmothers spirits, our culture can still be saved.

I feel to just ignore what has happened, would be our greatest defeat of all."

"Does any of this give you meaning young one?"

"Oh yes, for sure. I could listen to you all day Grey Wolf you have taught me so much over the years and there is so much more that I would like to learn. That is if you will teach me? I just feel hurt inside knowing now what us white folks did to your people."

"Don't feel hurt young one, as it wasn't you, it was a different time with different people. Also I should say in all sincerity young one, I do not teach. I just pass on what was shown to me by the Elders and if you are to learn from these things so be it. I can not take credit for what has been shown to our people for many years by the Great Spirit, that would not be right."

"Well then Grey Wolf, maybe you can then show me what I need to know. I sure would like to know more about your ways."

"So be it then young one, as time moves on and I think our days together are short."

"Short" I asked. "Are you going to leave the cottage Grey Wolf?"

"Not for awhile young one, but your road of life will change in the near future not mine. I can not talk more on the subject, but there is much to be learned.

To start off with you now know why I like to live here alone at this cottage by the water. I enjoy the quietness, the peacefulness of being alone. But even I have a weakness young one?"

"You do? What would that be?"

"You young one, you are my weakness, each day I yearn for your company and am saddened when you leave. But that is something for me not to dwell on, what is important, is to enjoy the time we both have right here an now."

48

I gotta' tell ya, when he told me that my eyes filled up and I had a hard time not showing it. Just before I left he gave me something to think on and asked that when I returned another day to share my thoughts.

"To understand what the Great Spirit is showing you young one, you have to open your mind. As you open your mind you also must feel within your heart what is happening in and around you. You have to realize that you are alive and being alive is not to do nothing, it's a time for you to explore all that has been given to you, and once done you will find the true meaning of life itself.

Today folks minds have been infected with things you see, material items like what you wear and illusionary things, like how you got it, and what you do for a living. Greed and selfishness has destroyed many a good man, young one, and listening to these things in your mind only clouds what is important. It limits you to what you are capable of really doing.

So young one, that is enough, as I can see your mind is full. Go now, and I look for your return."

Grey Wolf was a man of vision, his wisdom was shared with me, and my words today are shared with you. I know there is for some, reservations on my thinking, which is fine. I just think that in our material consciousness, that our lives of existence have been made so easy by technology, that our human struggle to do the right thing is shutting down.

Helpful Hints-To Drive Away Flees. Sprinkle a bit of lavender about the beds and other places they infest.

Hard Lessons

Years ago going to market with my old Dad sure added a lot of good memories to my story writing. The best part about the two day trip was being alone with my Dad, as he would get to tellin' stories and I just couldn't get enough of them. Most older folks had a way of getting the message across to younger folks back then. They didn't just come out and tell the young ones what to do, when to do it, or how it should be done, no sir. For most parts they would take a piece of their life and tell you a bit about it and if you listened close, each story had a message in it. Once they got finished telling you the story, what ever your problem was, well you felt better knowing that some one else had went through the same thing, or adventure in life as you did. A fellow or gal then knew how to deal with the problem. I suppose I got most of my education from my elders and today looking back I don't regret not having the diploma hanging on the wall one bit. It's only a paper my old Dad used to say, only a paper.

Old Grey Wolf my native friend always said, " young one, your knowledge will come from life experience's and it will do you well in your journey through life." He was so right, as relating back most things of importance I heard in stories from my elders, spared me from a lot of grief.

On this trip to market I was to learn a lesson on wild animals. Just one of many that was to follow later on. For a few years along an old highway, in a small town there used to be a gas station that we

stopped off at once in awhile to fill up the truck with gas, along with a soda for us.

While there, we got to noticing this cage off to the one side of the building. I walked over and inside was this old black bear. He sure looked sad thinking back. I asked the owner and he said he had found him as a cub and kept him. I asked him why he didn't let it go back to the wild, but he said he made money on wrestling the old bear while folks watched. I got to say being so young, it sure got my attention and I bugged my old Dad till he gave me a quarter, as that was what the owner wanted to go into the cage with the bear. I paid the man and in he went. The old bear stood up on his back feet and for a few minutes they went at it. Finally out he came and I was in awe that this fellow did what he did. I sure wouldn't have gone in there that's for darn sure.

We talked a bit more and then headed on down the highway. I got to talking about the incident to my Dad and he didn't say too much, I knew something was bothering him.

"Whats wrong I asked?"

"Well," he said, "I got to say I don't really think that old feller is doing the right thing keeping that bear caged up all these years. It's one thing to help it while it was young and lost from its mother, but it's another to keep it caged up and make money from it, in the way he has been doing. I know one has to do what he has to do, but he is really doing pretty well with just his gas station. Anyways that's my feelings." I never said much more, but the more I thought about it the more I agreed. When I told Grey Wolf a few years later, he said he should never have kept the old bear caged up, as something bad will come of it some day.

Years after that trip to market and I grew up some, I got to talking to Dad about what happened to the old bear.

"Well," he said, "it seems that the owner one day went in to fight the bear like he has done for so many years, but this time it was different. The old bear took offense of being caged up.

The story goes, that the bear killed the fellow with one swipe to his head. He then knocked down the cage door and let out for the bush out back and was never seen again." Hmm I thought, I guess the old bear had enough of being treated so badly and solved his problem himself, as a matter of fact just like Grey Wolf said would happen."

"Yep looks that way," said Dad, "hard lesson was learned there. He should have never kept the old bear caged up as he did, as nature has a way of looking after its own. Kind of like you and me I suppose, only difference is I try and direct you in the right direction before you make them mistakes, like my Dad did for me."

A hug was in order, I thought, and proceeded to put my arms around my old Dad's neck.

Helpful Hints-To Clean A Sponge. Rub fresh lemon juice thoroughly into a soured sponge, then rinse several times with warm water and the sponge will be as sweet as when new.

Paths We Choose

You know I believe the paths in ones life has been set, thing is it all depends on whether we gain enough wisdom to follow the right one.

This story was told to me by my old Grandfather, whom by the way had the same name as I do, George.

"It started on a cool fall afternoon, I had taken a job in helping to put through a highway in northern Ontario, up near our hometown of New Liskeard. I was operating an old D 9 Dozer, it was quite a machine back then but sure not compared to the ones of today. The rest of the crew had left for the weekend and I decided to work a bit late. I was pushing some big old pines out of the way, when not more than twenty feet in front of me, sat this old Indian on a log. I could see he wasn't going to move so I cut the engine and got off. I walked over to the old feller and told him that he would have to move so he wouldn't get hurt. He didn't say too much right off, but in a few minutes he looked up at me and said. "No highway going through here." I knew this couldn't be true as there was a lake on each side of us and there was no way we could go around, this was the only route.

"Well." I asked, "I am not sure what your reason is wanting to stop this operation, but how about you telling me why you don't want this road to go through."

"Road can not go through, my Grandfather is sleeping over there by that tree."

"What do you mean sleeping? I don't see anyone." It took a few minutes but then with teary eyes he told me the story of his Grandfather and how he was heading to a spot about sixty miles from here. He was old and not well and this spot he choose was when he was young, he tried his hardest to reach it as it was to be his final resting place, this was as far as he got."

Well I could see that this was going to pose a problem for our crew, so I said I would see what I could do. Ended up I talked the crew into letting me see if I could talk the fellow into letting me move his Grandfather to his final resting spot. Took me the better part of the day to convince him, but he agreed. A day later we had all the remains gathered up and started by horse back to the spot that he had mentioned. Took us another day to find the spot. Once there, we put up some posts and built a platform well up above the ground. While I worked on that, Red Hawk was his name, got to wrapping the remains in cloth. It was then placed on the platform and tied down. This is how we left the feller, not my way of doing things, but it wasn't up to me.

Back at the camp, or should say just a few miles before, the old Indian said. "I owe you a great deal of thanks friend and for your help and compassion I will tell you a bit of what is to come in your life. First you yourself will have a long, healthy, prosperous life, you will also be surrounded by folks that care for you. Later on you will have three sons and two daughters, the one son will have another son and daughter and that son will have two other sons. Them boys will be most important, they will have a life that isn't easy but with your wisdom and others, they will become men of wisdom beyond their years and will share that wisdom with words to those that so choose to listen.

One of your sons boys is special, different than most and in his later days he will spread the word of what has happened here on this day along with many others tales.

Well the road did go through and all was well.

"The thing though George, that got to me the most, was this. All he predicted to me throughout my life has happened and I am only sorry for one thing."

"What's that," I asked?

"I am sorry that I won't be around to see the ending and how you go through your life. I guess it will be through your eyes to see if it all happens as he said."

Well you know at the time I didn't give it much thought, actually no thought, until one night I was laying in bed and this story came to mind. I had an uncontrollable urge to get up and write a few things down which I did.

54

Kind of gets a fellow to thinking doesn't it? Reason being, this old Indian was able to see the future and the different paths that were already chosen.

I only have this to add, he was right in his predictions, my life wasn't easy. But thinking back I had good folks looking out for me and I did listened to the wisdom that came to me, along with putting that wisdom into finding, The Paths We Choose.

Helpful Hints-To Remove Bad Smells From Clothing.
Articles of clothing or any other articles which have bad smelling substances on them, may be freed from smell by wrapping them up lightly and burying them in the ground for a day or two.

Hats & Things

My old Dad used to say. "George, you can always tell a man by the kind of hat he wears. For years I didn't really give it much thought, but now looking back I see it did have some substance.

For example, back on the farm when one was out in the fields in the summer time, you would never see a farmer without a straw hat. In the winter he would wear wool of some kind or felt. The change in the hats came in the late 1900's when they introduced the baseball caps.

Thinking about that I can't for the life of me see why, as they don't do much in shading a fellow in hot weather. They also don't do much to help a fellow keep dry when a heavy rain starts to fall and they sure don't help with a persons appearance. Or at least not compared to the western look through my eyes.

Years ago the cowboy hat made a person, meaning it gave them a good feeling inside when wearing one. Guess you could say it made them feel proud. I kind of think the best way of comparing the hats of today with the hats of times past, would be like a bicycle. Yep a bicycle, years ago they made bicycles with fenders that stopped the water from being thrown up on ones self, kept one dry. They also had a bell or a horn on them to let folks know they were around. Even had a light which generated its own power and lasted for years. Today it's just the opposite, folks pay ten times as much as they use to for the things and only get half the bike.

Strange how things have changed like that. Some say it's progress, but I say it's just in how one looks at it. I guess it all boils down to how much one has to spend.

For years on the farm one made do with things and when something went wrong they repaired them, had to, as there was just no money to buy new. Hand me downs was a big thing back then. I remember some folks up the road from us that had a large family, six girls and five boys. The youngest one said she never owned a new pair of jeans till she married and moved away from the farm. Gets me to smiling every time I think of that.

Getting back to the old straw and felt hats, it was kind of like that with them too. Thing one has to remember though is that things lasted a long time back then. Reason being they were made a lot better. Myself when it comes to a hat I still like to buy the Stetson. I don't think there is a better made hat anywhere on the planet and looks, well, it's kind of like that song I heard awhile back from a country singer that sang, My Baby's Got Her Blue Jeans On. Turns heads in the right direction and not to forget all the other benefits it brings a fellow or gal. The old Bailey hats are pretty good too.

Yep I am from the old school as you can tell and nothing will ever change that. Not that I can't change, just that I don't want to, as I enjoy the way I am.

Last, remembering back, my old Dad used to say, "George there is a lot of folks out there that can look ahead in life, but the secret to bringing it all together, is being able to see things. Kind of like a team of horses. Horses are smart critters as they not only look, they see, that's why they put blinders on them back then, so they would do just what the old farmer wanted them to do, not what they wanted to do."

Hmm, kind of gets me to thinking of what's happening in today's world.

Helpful Hints-To Keep Wooden Pails an Tubs From Shrinking. Soak them with glycerin and the wooden pails and tubs will not shrink and fall to pieces.

Have You
Learned Anything

Growing up, I can always remember Laura asking at the end of each day if I had learned anything. One day I asked her what she meant by that and she said. "Well George, no matter what you do or where you go throughout a day you should always be learning something. For example when you went for that ride with Jennie, *Jennie is my horse*, this morning did you learn anything while you were on your ride.

Well I thought about that for a minute and then said. "Not that I remember, nope I guess I didn't. Was I suppose to?"

"Yep you should have, so how about you going for another ride and this time see what you can learn and let me know when you return. I got some work to do anyways, so this will give you something to do."

Well I thought, I guess I could, not sure though what I am looking for but I will give it a try, besides Jennie always liked to go for rides, no matter how many times a day.

I walked over to the barn, called Jennie in from the field, saddled up and was off. At first I just rode along trying to figure out in my

mind exactly what Laura meant, or what I should be looking for. Then after a bit I started to look around a bit more. First off all I noticed was the birds flying here and there as I passed them by. I then told Jennie to hold up there a minute and just watched them. I soon seen that they were not just playing like I thought they were doing, they were gathering food like seeds and berries. Once they collected the food I watched what they did with it and found they hid it in cracks of trees and buried some at the base of trees. That told me they were putting it away for safe keeping for a later date.

Hmm I thought, there is lots I can learn if I just take the time to look around a bit and not be in such a hurry. I then got down from Jennie and went over to a log and sat down for a bit. As I sat there I watched Jennie as she had wondered over to a tree and rubbed up against it with the back of her neck. She then put her head down and started to feed off of some of the grass. Just watching her gave me a good feeling inside, relaxed me you might say. I noticed how she moved the older dead grass away with her nose to get to the nice green stuff. She sure wasn't no dumb animal.

As she ate I noticed her every so often lift her head and smell the air. Then at that instance, her ears went back, her tail went up and she snorted out loud. Looking around I then noticed over to the right of me near the base of a large pine, that a wolf was standing there watching us. Jennie had spotted him and was now keeping an eye on him. After a bit the wolf up and left, probably figuring his cover was found out, so no use hanging around. After a few minutes Jennie put her head back down and went back to her eating. So I thought, if when alone, one just kept an eye on their horse, they would know when danger was close by, as the horse would warn them. Darn I thought, Laura was right, I am learning new things and all that it took was paying a bit more attention to what was going on around me.

On the way out of the bush I looked up into the sky noticing how blue it was. Boy I thought, it sure is a great day. With that I reached down and patted Jennie on the neck.

"You know girl, I guess we got to pay a bit more attention to things around us when we go riding from now on. Never know what we might learn." With that Jennie just threw her head back as if it say.

"That's what I have been trying to tell ya, just that you haven't been listening to me." With that we headed on back home.

At home I unsaddled Jennie, gave her a bit of a rub down, a handful of oats and mosied on over to the house. Soon as I entered the door Laura asked. "So did you..."

"Yep sure did," I said, before she could get the sentence finished. "I learned lots," and proceeded to tell her all about it. She smiled and said. "There you go, now you know what I was trying to get across to

you. I could have just told you, but by you finding it out on your own, it will stay with you now for the rest of your life"

You know thinking about that, it has stayed with me, as now no matter where I go, or what I do, I always make sure I learn something along the way. Thing is, that after one does it a few times, it just becomes second nature.

So there you go, a bit on how one young feller got to learning a few things throughout his life without having to go to school.

Helpful Hints-To Temper Lamp Chimneys And Other Glassware. Put them into cold water; bring slowly to the boiling point and let them boil for an hour. They should be allowed to cool before removing them from the water.

Hot Day
On The Old Farm

It was a hot summers day and Reg and myself had been out in the fields.
We grew mostly corn, because we had cattle to feed along with some oats but it wasn't a big thing, because the after product of the oats is straw, isn't much good for anything but bedding for the critters, but it was a necessity. Haying was the big time of the year and Reg always said once that was over with he could sit back and enjoy his old pipe for the rest of the year. Not really though in my mind, as we were always busy doing something. One thing about farm living there is never an idle moment.

Sundays though were a day of rest, other than milking and cleaning out the stalls. On this day though it was a hot one, so hot we decided to call it quits for awhile, till the sun got more over into the west.

"So what are you going to do, for the rest of the afternoon," Reg asked, speaking to me.

"Well I would sure love to have some ice cream, but Laura said we don't have any more ice left in the ice house."

"Well, said Reg, "one needs ice for ice cream, hmm....let me think."
He took off his old Stetson and sat down on a rock which made up a
fence line.

"You know, last fall I was out cutting firewood and came across this
old cave. If I remember correctly, inside there was ice way back in
aways, hanging from the ceiling. What do you say we go and take a
look?"

"Sounds good to me," I said and off we went.

Didn't take us long and soon we came upon the cave. In we went
and just as Reg had said, inside way back in was all the ice we needed.
I remember it like yesterday, just hanging there, had a clear bluish
ting to it. I broke off a big piece and just let it melt in my mouth.

"Boy, I said, that sure feels and tastes great."

We had brought an old bushel with us and we loaded it up and
headed on back to the house. Laura greeted us at the door.

"Laura, remember the other day. You said we could make ice cream
if we had ice, well look here what Reg and me got?"

"Well I'll be," she said, "I guess we will have to get to making some
then won't we. You get out the ice cream maker and wash it out a bit.
Reg you break up the ice and get the rock salt and I will get the cream
from this mornings milking, good thing I kept some."

Reg and I did what we were told and in no time we were all set to
get to the making part. First we put some salt in, then some crushed
ice, then more salt, then finished filling it with more ice.

Laura dumped in the cream and said. "Get to turning, as it is going
to take a bit of work as you know."

"No problem," I said, as I knew what the finished product was
going to be.

I turned the old crank on the ice cream maker for a bit first, then
Reg spelled me and after that Laura finished things up. Just before it
was done she took off the lid and dumped in some fresh strawberries
mixed with some raspberries. I got to tell ya, did we have a treat.
There is nothing in my way of thinking, that is so tasty as fresh ice
cream, made using fresh cream, you have never lived till you have
tried it.

We then headed out to the front porch with our bowls full to the
brim. As I sat there I got to thinking.

"You know Reg and Laura, life can't get much better than this can
it?"

"Nope," they both said, "it sure can't."

While telling that story it got me to thinking about an old ice cream
maker a lady here in Port Loring had. It was all apart and not worth
too much anymore, but I had written a story awhile back about
making homemade ice cream and she called me up and said I could

have the old thing if I wanted it. Well I took it and put it back together, took some doing but end results it turned out not too bad.

Right now I have it sitting here by the kitchen door and just looking at it got me to thinking about writing this story. Also got me thinking that I might just get to making some homemade ice cream too. We do have some fresh strawberries and raspberries in the freezer, why not, it will be just like stepping back in time.

In closing, I would also like to say thanks to the lady who gave me that old machine, it meant a lot to me and will be around for years to come.

Helpful Hints-To Soften Water. Boil a small bottle in a kettle to soften water. The carbonate of lime and other impurities will be found adhering to the bottle.

How One Learns

In my younger days I can still hear Laura and Reg saying.

"Early to bed and early to rise, makes you healthy wealthy and wise." Now I am not saying that putting them three words into practice has helped me get wealthy, but I do know that over the years my family and I have been blessed with pretty good health for most parts. Being wise, I guess I would have to say was gained over time. So two out of three I can't complain.

It wasn't just time though that brought on wisdom, it was what one did with the time. An example would be, Reg, Laura, my Dad or Grey Wolf sitting with me on a summers evening outdoors and tellin' me about their past life experiences.

Many an evening was passed with them sharing their wisdom and filling my head with all kinds of things, which would be taken to bed for me to think on. Sometimes after listening to them older folks I would lay in bed for hours, my mind just a racing to find answers to the things that were bothering me. Only to find out that the answers to my problems had already been solved, in a story that had been told to me at an earlier time.

I guess you could say I was lucky in sort, compared to what we have today, as even though I didn't have my birth parents raise me, I did have a family just as worthy, maybe more so, as they taught me about love, kindness and all kinds of things that a young boy needed to know.

Another saying was the early bird gets the worm and I have found that saying to be so true, especially at breakfast time. Reason being, I

found that if I got to the table before Reg got there, I got the pick of the flapjacks or bacon. Was hard to do though, as he was up before daylight.

I guess that is why you hear the birds a chirping so early in the mornings, as those up first are sure of a full tummy for the rest of the day.

Many a mornings even before the sun was awake I could be found sitting at the kitchen table listening to a neighbor that had dropped by for a visit talking to Reg and Laura about what they were going to do that day.

Things were explained back then in full detail so that anyone of any age could understand their meanings. Guess you could say the words them older folks choose to use had knowledge built in them, just waiting for you to go out and use.

I can remember Reg, Laura and myself talking till the yellow rays of the sun made its presence through our kitchen window and me wanting it never to end. Just couldn't take in enough of what they were saying, always learning, wanting to know more. I would have to say I learned just as much from them as I did at school, maybe more.

Back then we didn't have a newspaper, television to find out things. What one learned was strictly from others, or as some would say, I learned the hard way. In other words one took things upon themselves to try on their own, sometimes they worked, other times they didn't. The thing was one didn't get to frettin' if something didn't work out, nope, they learned by their mistakes and went on to trying different things and thought up different ideas. Might say they used their minds to the fullest.

Today lookin' back, pretty well everyone I ever knew made out pretty darn good throughout their life and left their young ones and others a good world to live in.

Most folks today don't think or do things like we did back then, as we have machines to do our thinking and physical labor for us. If one would ask me personally to choose between yesteryear and todays world. Without hesitation I would tell them, I would probably not change anything, as the bad and hard times made the good times more enjoyable.

If there was any words of wisdom that I could offer you, it would be these.

"If you get up at dawn, work hard every day, eat healthy and smile, good things will happen."

Helpful Hints-To Keep Cranberries. Put them into a keg of water and they may be kept all winter.

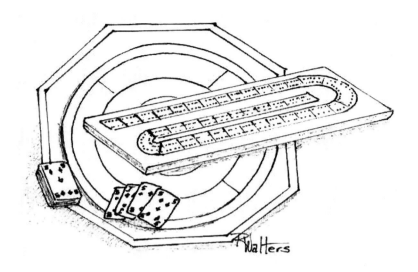

It's All In How You Hold Them

I know most of you folks have played a hand of cards in your day and probably a few will be able to relate with this tale.

In my teens, later on in life, my old Dad bought some property down in the sunny south, just south of Sarasota on the old Tamiami Trail or some called it highway 41. I think I remember my Dad saying they started building that road in 1915, bet it could tell a few stories in itself huh? For years we went there and eventually even built a cottage on a few acres my Dad had boughten, wrote a story about building it in one of my other books. The thing about them days I remember the most, was some of the friends I made. Jerry was one fellow, his mother rented a place next door and over the years we became good friends. Vi his mother also became a good friend and right up until she passed away we were always in touch. I have to say though, it sure is hard even thinking of Florida without her being there anymore.

But as I said, Jerry and I became good friends not to forget Jerry's brother Bill and quite often in the evening hours we would get to playing cards. We sure had some good times.

Our favorite card game was Euchre and soon as the dishes were put away, out would come the cards. Sometimes even when we were eating, a few hands would be dealt. Jerry and myself were inseparable in the beginning until he moved away, then Bill came into the picture.

Most of the time in the beginning Jerry and myself would be partners and my Dad and Vi would be partners. You have to really watch in that game, especially back then as we were young and they, meaning Vi and Dad were old, or so to speak. I am not saying these older folks would count any extra points unknowingly but seemed to Jerry and I, we were always loosing. For those that know the game you can count with twos and threes, or at least we do, but some count with two fives. Simple enough it would seem, but my old Dad being a farmer, he likes to sprout them a wee bit every now and then, saying it brought good luck. Again I am not saying he was cheating, but seems to me them sprouts grew pretty fast sometimes.

So in seeing this Jerry and I came up with our own little bit of help. Like coughing real hard, kicking each other in the leg, moving our left ear, and one of our favorites, do you want another drink, coke or cream soda. In other words make it black or red. We didn't make a habit out of it, just that these older folks were so darn good at what they were doing, well we figured it would give us an edge.

Thing is though, even with all these things we figured out, they still managed to beat us most of the time. Never could figure that out, I kind of think now, maybe them two had a few things worked out between themselves, either that or we played so many games they just knew us better than we knew each other.

I can also say, in all the games of Euchre we played and that was thousands, there was never any arguing. We had so many laughs that at the end of the night we all had sore sides. I sure miss them old days.

Another game my Dad and I played a lot, was Crib. I remember we used to drive him south, my wife and I when he was getting older so he could have his car, stay a few weeks and then fly home. On the way down in the motel, we were no sooner in the door of our room and out would come the crib-board.

"Lets get a game started, before supper," he would say. Sometimes it got me a wee bit upset, but probably just because I was a bit hungry, I didn't say anything though, as I knew how much he loved to play.

What would I give now for a game or two with him. Makes me sad in some ways when I think of my old Dad, being gone an all, but in others, well lets just say I have fond memories. And call on them some days I do, especially when my path in life throws me a few curves.

Where we live now, my wife and I have a lot more free time, or should say we make more free time and at our table at any given day, there is a crib game going on. Lately though we have been playing crib in the mornings, an on going game and crokinole at lunch, as I came

across an old crokinole board, great game too and couldn't have spent a better five dollars in all my born days.

Well there you go, a bit about how we had fun years ago and even into today. Try it sometime, sure beats watching television every night and on the plus side, it brings a Husband and Wife and family, closer together, something we could all use a bit more of in this busy old world. "Don't ya think?"

Helpful Hints-To Keep Onions. The best way is to spread them over the floor.

Laura's Apron

"**G**eorge when you get the firewood brought in for the cook stove saddle up Jennie and take a ride over to Mrs. Anderson's, as she made me a new apron a month ago and I haven't had time to go and get it yet." I didn't mind as I loved to go for a ride with Jennie.

A few minutes later I had Jennie saddled up and was on my way. The way to Mrs. Anderson's could be gotten to by the road but I didn't like going that way, as Jennie didn't like cars or trucks that much, made her kind of fidgety.

The way I liked to go was through the bush as there was an old logging road from years past and it was sure pretty back there. Jennie loved it too, as with all the other critters running around and different smells it kept her head just a moving, she didn't miss a thing.

An hour or so later I arrived at Mrs. Anderson's, she was sittin' on the front porch darning up a pair of socks, probably her husbands.

As I got nearer she looked up and said. "Well hello there stranger what brings you to this neck of the woods?

"Came to pick up Laura's new apron you made for her."

"Well it's about time, I had it ready for her for over a month now. At any rate get down off Jennie there, tie her up by the apple tree as there is a few apples that has fallen on the ground. I am sure she will enjoy them along with the shade from the tree."

I did what I was told and then sat down beside Mrs. Anderson on an old box that was sitting up against the wall.

We talked a bit and then she got up and got me a cool drink of lemonade and brought out the apron.

"Sure looks pretty," I said, "and one thing is for sure, Laura sure needs one as hers is about worn out. Beats me why she wears it so much."

"You know George an apron is not just a pretty item for a lady to wear, it has many uses. The main reason I guess would be to protect her dress from getting dirty, as most women including myself don't have but one or two and we like to keep them as long as possible.

Also aprons don't take too much material when it comes to making them, not like a dress and material is hard to come by these days.

It also comes in really handy for taking the pots and things out of the oven or from the top of the stove, saved many a burned hand let me tell you. Now can you think of anything that you seen Laura using hers for?"

"Hmm, well I have had her wipe a tear or two from my eyes when I got hurt now and then, along with when I was really young it was a good place to hide when strangers came for a visit. At least till I got to know them better.

Oh and she uses it quite a bit to put the eggs in when she goes to the chicken coop, along with that I have seen her many a days wiping her brow while cooking with it.

As a matter of fact just before I came over here I was bringing in firewood for the cook stove and she helped me a bit by bringing in some kindlin' which she used her apron to carry it with. Now that I think of it, she uses it for a lot of things."

"Yes us women sure do make good use of them, there are all kinds of things we use them for. Myself when I go to the garden I use it to bring in my vegetables, along with carrying a few apples that has fallen from our tree over there."

"Oh ya," I said, "Laura does that too and when unexpected company comes she sure puts that apron to work dusting things, let me tell ya. Not to forget the new born kittens yesterday, as they were cold and she wrapped them up in her apron to get warm while waiting for their mother to get back from hunting up a mouse in the barn."

A bit more was said that day, I carefully put the new apron in my saddle bags so it wouldn't get dirty, said goodbye and left for home.

Along the way home the more I thought about Laura's apron the more I realized just how important it really was. I guess you could compare it to the old handkerchief that was used years ago. As it had many a use too, still does for me even today.

No Sir, Laura wouldn't have been Laura without her apron, as even today when thinking of her, the first thing that comes to mind, is her

standing over the old cook stove wiping her hands on her apron saying.

"George....get them hands of yours washed, supper will be on the table in a few minutes." With that I would do as she said and when all done washing, yep I dried my hands on her apron.

Helpful Hints-To Keep All Kinds Of Herbs. Just before or while the herbs are in blossom gather them on a dry day, tie in bundles and hang up with the blossoms downward. When they are perfectly dry those that are to be used as medicine, should be wrapped in paper and kept from the air, while those that are to be used in cooking, should have the leaves picked off, pounded sifted fine, and put in tightly sealed bottles.

Helpful Hints-The Temperature That Vegetables Should Be Kept. Vegetables should be kept at as low a temperature as possible without freezing. Apples will stand a very low temperature but sweet potatoes should have a dry and warm atmosphere and should be packed in dry leaves. Squashes should be kept in a dry place and as cool as possible without freezing.

Helpful Hints-To Keep Vegetables. If they are to be kept a long time they should be pulled on a dry day and the tops should be cut off and trimmed. Pack them in layers in barrels or boxes with moss or dry straw between and over them. The moss keeps them from shriveling yet keeps out any excess moisture.

Not To Be Taken Lightly

I gotta' say some of us older folks have a different way of lookin' at things. Reason being is that some of us had different upbringings. I for one was very lucky in having a couple that took me in and raised me to what I am today, and I would have to say that they did a heck of a good job.

I can always remember Laura, no matter where we went, always either telling me something, or showing me something. For example, one day we were out walking, she stopped and said. "Do you happen to notice anything where we are standing George?" I thought about it for a bit, looked around to see if I was missing something, then said.

"Nope don't see nothin' different."

"Well, she said, "close your eyes and let your nose see if it can detect anything."

With that I closed my eyes and for the life of me I couldn't smell anything. "Nope can't smell anything out of the ordinary."

"Out of the ordinary," she said, "what would that be?"

"Something that hasn't always been there I guess," I replied.

"Exactly, now close your eyes again and tell me what you smell that has always been there." So I did, and the only thing I could smell was the trees.

"I guess it would have to be the cedars that I smell the most right now."

"Exactly, that is what I smell too and it tells you that cedars are near by."

"I reckon," I said, "but what can I learn from that, as they are always there, don't mean nothing, does it?"

"It does mean something George. It means that you are passing things by in your everyday life and not even noticing them. That is not a good thing, as it means that you are just taking things for granted, and life is much more than that. You should be aware of everything and everybody that is around you at all times, as it will save you a lot of grief in your coming years, along with giving you, wealth and happiness. Not only that, but if you keep working on all your senses like smell, hearing, feelings and things, they will then automatically do it on their own. Something like you are doing right now, but instead of just automatically passing things by, you will notice them. I have always found it is better knowing, than not knowing what lies around the next bend.

Life is full of learning George and the only one that can up grade your senses is you. I can make you aware of what has to be done, but after that it is up to you."

You know for years after that Laura and Reg showed and brought things to my attention, and now here today, no matter where I go or what I do they are automatically picked up by my mind.

For example one time my wife and I was out for a walk which we do quite regularly. I should mention that we live here in the north surrounded by bush and wild life. Probably more wild life than humans at this point. At any rate, we were out for a walk and all of a sudden I stopped, as a smell came floating to me on the wind. My wife asked what I stopped for, and I told her that I could smell a deer or moose close by. Sure enough after looking around we found where they had bedded down for the night amongst some cedars.

These smells were brought back from my teachings of years past, as when Reg and I were out hunting one day we came upon a couple deer and Reg brought to my attention what they smelled like. So you might say I put it away in my mind bank and now when ever I come across that smell it stops me and gets me to lookin' around.

What good will these things do me in my every day life some ask? Well, I think my dearest friend old Grey Wolf can sum it up with these words that he told me many years ago.

"You know George, lessons for the young is to talk, think less and observe more. This will help in developing the habit of reading the secret language of nature."

The Good Old Days

No denying things have changed over the years that's for sure, but ensuring that them thoughts are never lost, I thought I would put together a few items, places and times that once was.

I still can remember opening up the underside of pop caps to see if I won anything. If I was really lucky a free trip to the movie theater would be in order. Sure enjoyed them Saturday afternoons out with my friends. I still can smell the pop corn, not to forget the taste of the sodas and hot dogs.

Sitting around the kitchen table at noon or in the evenings also was quite an event, as not only did we have a meal of home cookin' but I got to listen to our old Philco Radio. Some of the shows were Amos & Andy, Gunsmoke and the Shadow. For most parts I liked them all, but Gunsmoke and the Shadow were my favorites.

I also had a yearning to collect comic books back then and sure wished now I had saved all that I collected over the years. Could have probably retired on what they would be worth today.

Some that I enjoyed were the good old Western Comics, Action Comics, Danial Boone, Davey Crockett, Gunsmoke, Treasure Island, White Fang, Jughead, Detective Comics and last but not least, The Last Of the Mohican's, all were a great way for me to escape from the

hustle an bustle around me. A place where all was possible and excepted in the mind of a young boy.

Eventually the old record player or as some would call them, the Hi-Fi was born and the 45's and L P's were being sold everywhere. I just couldn't get enough and I must say I had quite a collection of different singers. Some would be, Buddy Holly & The Crickets, Ritchie Valens, Dion & The Belmonts and the Big Bopper.

I can still see myself sittin' down town in Guelph many years ago at a small restaurant. On one side was booths which one could set in, and an old Juke Box which sat up against another wall, playing the golden oldies. The girls all had ponytails and wore long poodle skirts and saddle shoes.

Myself along with other boys had our hair slicked back with Brylcreem, wore blue jeans, white T-shirts and for a jacket, well....one will never forget the good old black leather jacket, it was like a second skin.

Some of the treats in my early days were to die for, like Black Jack and Beemans gum, not to forget good old Bazooka bubble gum which was quite a hit with the gals. Once in awhile I got a Sugar Daddy caramel sucker or two, which I could make last for a whole day.

Coke in a bottle for 5 cents was up there on top of the list and you would never see anyone at their favorite restaurant down town without a bottle sitting in front of them.

After a day out with my friends one would come home to watch his favorite TV show on the old black and white television set. To name a few would be, The Honeymooners, Gunsmoke, Bonanza, Ed Sullivan, My Friend Flica, Red Skelton, Wagon Train, Jack Benny, Ozzie & Harriet, Sky King and my most favorite Your Hit Parade. I gotta' say, some of the singers they had on there sure could sing up a storm.

Yes those were the days. Oh can't forget Christmas, as it was one time of the year that us young ones sure looked forward to. Some of the toys I got were. A Lionel Train Set, Tinker Toys, Erector Sets, Lincoln Logs, the good old Slinky, Hula Hoops, Frisbee and an Ant Farm. Oh can't forget my Mickey Mouse Ears or my old Coonskin Hat. Darn sure miss them too, guess the boy never really leaves the man huh?

Cars now was something that not too many young folks had, but the ones that was lucky enough to have enough money to buy one, well....lets just say they were in high demand. Some of the old cars that I loved were; the old 58 Edsel, and I had one too. The old Studebaker was kind of on the low down side of things, or that is what us younger ones thought at the time. Top of the line in cars was the 57 Chevy and my most favorite my 57 Ford. Now there was a car. Many a nights we visited the old Drive In Theater let me tell ya.

Talking about the Drive In, we sure had some good times. One of us guys would usually be put in the trunk to save a dollar, which was used for treats throughout the night.

After the movie we would all congregate at A&W as it was the place to be. Girls waited on you out by your car and I can't rightly recollect any boy back then not having a girl friend. If it wasn't A&W we would be at the Dairy Queen getting' served chocolate milkshakes and hot dogs.

For awhile there I even got into drag racing at the track on Saturday nights. Sure got the girls attention let me tell ya and yes I did do a bit down main street every so often too. Poor old police cars back then never seen us for dust. Still can see them hollering and trying to wave us down.

Gas back then was around 28 cents a gallon and it never ceased to amaze me that there was never a Friday or Saturday night that we didn't have enough cash to do our thing.

So there you go, a trip back to memory lane, when families pulled together, you could say a slower slice of life. When a bad day would consist of your parents finding out that you had played hooky from school. My how I dreaded to go home and face my old Dad on them days. Then to find out just how much he did love me by taking me to the old wood shed or grounding me for a week. Don't get me wrong, it didn't happen too often in my life and it wasn't because he didn't really love me, it was the way us young ones learned. Dad always said, there is a hard way of learning, or....an easy way, all up to you.

Today the bad things would be drive by shootings, drugs of all kinds, food not worth mentioning, well just too many to name. So...now when asked. Why George do you keep on writing about the old days? I say....take it from the top folks, and all will unfold before your eyes.

Helpful Hints-To Keep Peas For Winter Use. Shell them and put them into boiling water, with a little salt added, boil for five minutes. Drain in colander and afterwards on a cloth, then place in air-tight bottles. When used they should be boiled till tender and seasoned in butter.

Off To Market

I'll never forget one trip to market that my old Dad and I made. There were many but this one stands out in my mind.

Every week come Friday we would load the truck with fresh fruit and vegetables and head on up north to our farmers market. We would get there usually in the wee hours of the morning. On this trip though things were rolling right along without a care in the world one might say. Dad was telling me stories to pass the time while driving, and me, well I was all ears. About halfway I took out our thermos of coffee that was made for us before we left and poured Dad and myself a cup. I have to say that I sure enjoyed that part of the trip, as I didn't usually get coffee that often. Sure tasted good too.

Another thing I enjoyed about the trip was the smell of the old truck, along with all the fruit and things on the back. Occasionally even today I have encountered a few of them smells and when it happens I am brought to an abrupt halt, and instantly I am taken back in time. Amazing what just a smell or two can do in helping a fellow remember things.

Well I poured the coffee and handed a cup to my Dad. As he drove he sipped away at it saying. "Gall-darn-it George, this is the life huh? Can't get any better than this." Still hear his words even today, darn I sure miss him.

I was told one time along while ago, that our loved ones are never far away. They are always right there with you, you just have to talk to them. You would probably say that one is not right in their mind,

talking to something that can't be seen. For me though, I have to say that I've been doing it for years. Do I ever get an answer some have asked? Well, let me just say that I wouldn't be asking if I thought I wouldn't. The answer doesn't come to one through words though, you have to visualize who you are talking to, then and only then you will understand what they are telling you.

Quite a few hours later we were in the north and I spotted the turn off which would take us into town. Coming into town we had to pass a hospital for the mentally infirm, and right beside it up on a hill I heard a huge bang. The old truck swerved to the right. Dad was a strong man and he managed to get the truck off to the side of the road. We got out and found we blew a front tire.

"Well," said Dad, "guess we got some work to do."

"Yep looks that way," I said.

Dad got out the jack which he carried at all times and rolled the spare tire around to the front of the truck. Boy it was sure cold out there remembering back. But I knew as soon as the sun made its appearance, things would be seen with a whole new meaning. Dad then got to removing the nuts so we could get the tire off, while I kept him entertained with my chatting. Once off I rolled the flat tire back behind the truck, which wasn't an easy chore. But I managed it OK and got lots of praise from my old Dad.

I went back around to the front of the truck and where Dad had put the nuts for the front wheel, in the hub cap, I accidentally stepped on it flinging the nuts down the hill and into a ditch that was around five feet deep with water.

Now I am in trouble I thought, and I yes I did get hollered at. Well we were standing there when I noticed we weren't alone. From the hospital a young feller had come up on us and was watching. I looked at Dad and he looked at me and then we both looked at the young fellow, with Dad saying. "Where did you come from?"

The young fellow, replied and said. "Right over there," pointing to the hospital, "out for my morning stroll, airs not good in that place, folks in there say I am dumb, but I know different."

"Can't say I blame you," said Dad."

"So what are we going to do now?" I asked Dad.

"Well, guess I will have to go for a walk to town and see if I can buy some new lug nuts for the truck. It's about a half hour walk I would say. You will have to stay and keep an eye on the truck while I am gone."

That said the young feller from the hospital spoke up and asked, "Why?"

"Why what?" said my Dad.

"Why are you going to get some nuts for the truck, why walk all that way in the cold?"

"Well nothing else I can do, if I want to get this truck to rolling down the highway there young feller."

With that the young feller walked up and took my Dad by the arm, and pointed at the other wheels on the truck. "Why not just take one nut from each of the others, still enough to hold them on, more than enough, and save you walking all that way for nothing."

Well Dad looked at me and I looked at him and laughed.

"You know there young fellow, I don't think you need to be here in this hospital at all."

"I've been tellin' them that for the past two years mister," he replied. With that he mosied on his way.

"Kind of makes you think, huh George?"

"Sure does Dad, kind of makes one think who is the not so smart ones here."

With that we took off one nut from the three other wheels, and we were on our way. For years after that every time we passed the hospital Dad would look at me and I him and we both would let out a laugh, then saying.

"Wonder what ever happened to that young feller?"

Helpful Hints-To Keep Apples. Apples are usually kept on open shelves where any that begin decaying may be removed immediately. Sometimes they are packed in layers of dry sand but care should be taken that they do not touch each other. They also may be packed in any grain, such as oats, barley, etc. If the apples are very choice, each apple should be wrapped separately in paper and packed in a box.

Helpful Hints-To Keep Grapes. The simplest way is to keep them in drawers or boxes that holds twenty-five pounds each and pile them one above the other. Another way is to hang, like a barrel hoop from the ceiling by three cords; seal the stem with wax, attach a wire to the small end of the bunch and hang from the hoop, taking care that no two bunches touch. The imperfect grapes should previously been picked off. The room should be not too moist but yet not too dry as it will wither the grapes and it should be free from frost.

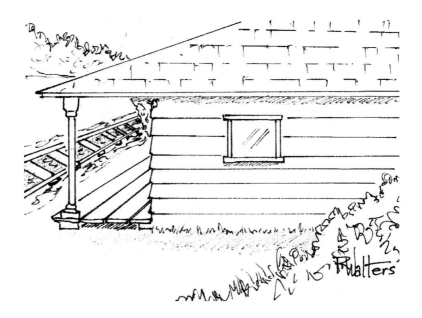

Pays To Think

Was a busy time of year on the farm, we had just brought in some peaches from the orchard and parked the tractor and trailer under a tree for shade.

Well," said Dad, "I think we are going to need some more baskets. I thought for sure we had enough for today, but I noticed that we are getting low."

We then both walked over to the truck and headed off down to the Basket Factory, which at that time was here in town. On our arrival they told us the baskets we needed, were being stored over in the old train station. I guess they must have been renting it from the town.

"Good idea," Dad said, "no use in the building just going to waste."

On hearing that, we got back in the truck and headed on over. Wasn't too far, would only take a few minutes. When there we went inside and Dad got to talking to the fellow that was in charge. He brought down the baskets and we carried them to the truck and while we were busy doing that, I listened as the fellow told Dad about this big old bee's nest that hung up under the front of the train station.

Huge thing he said and so far this year I got stung four times. Well Dad listened for a bit and a fellow that also lived there in town and some times a bit of a bragger decided to speak up. "If you have a problem with them bees, I can get rid of them for ya. Only take me a minute and they will be gone. Won't charge you that much either."

The fellow that worked at the station, looked at my Dad and I seen my Dad kind of shaking his head in disagreement. But the fellow being stung a few times said, "OK when can you do it?"

"I'll come by later on tonight, as the bees aren't out bothering a fellow at that time." They agreed and everyone went on their way.

Around nine that night we were all sitting around enjoying the evening, when we heard the fire department siren.

"Hmm, said Dad, wonder what's happening, maybe we should go and have a look, just in case we can be of some help." I asked if I could come and he said, "sure jump in."

Dad started the old truck and we headed on into town. Ahead of us we could see a huge red area that lite up the night sky.

"Fire looks like it's down by the railway tracks," Dad said.

"Yep sure does, I wonder what's happening?"

When there, we seen the whole train station was up in flames. They did their best in trying to put it out, but with no water readily available at that time, and the old station being so dry it was a loosing battle. Dad and me hung around a bit talking to folks, when Dad asked one of the fireman how it got started.

He just looked at Dad and said. "Well Sir, you won't believe this, but a fellow here in town decided he was going to get rid of a bees nest, that has been pestering the fellow that worked here."

"What's that got to do with a fire Dad asked?"

"Well the feller, decided he would light up a torch, hold it under the hive and burn the thing. Not a good idea though, as above the hive they stored straw and well a spark got in there and in an instant the whole darn place went up. With all them wood baskets and straw, it was just impossible to put it out. Just had to kind of watch and let it burn."

"Son of a gun," Dad said, "I over heard them talking earlier today and I kind of thought he might try and do something crazy. I maybe should have tried to steer them in a different direction when I was here. Too late now though."

Well, we talked a bit more and headed on home, as not much more could be done. What was done was done.

"Amazing how some folks think, said Dad. "Why in tar nation, would a fellow hold a torch up under a roof, loaded with old dry baskets and straw. I got to tell you George, it just goes to show you, how not thinking things out, can sure cause a mess of trouble. So there you have it, the night we lost the Old Train Station.

Only one good thing came out of the whole mess. "Got rid of the Bees."

Slowing Down

Times has changed over the years and an interesting thing is the change in the pace. Fifty years ago it was the pace of a horse walking. Now it is as fast as a car or truck can go. Thinking back some of the problems weren't high tech as in todays world, but in saying that, they were still important and had to be dealt with. One that I remember quite well was to do with our laying hens.

I remember Laura saying one day. "Reg, them hens aren't laying as they used to and I am not sure why. Usually if they stop laying they will start moulting first, then go off laying slowly, but lately instead of getting three or four dozen eggs a day, we are only getting around six or seven, if this keeps up we won't have enough for breakfast." I have to say that sure got Reg's attention, as he loved his bacon and eggs in the morning.

"That's strange," said Reg, "something must be happening that we aren't seeing. George, today I want you to do some detective work and keep an eye on them old hens and see if you can find out what's happening to them."

"No problem," I said and headed on out to the barn.

For about three days I kept an eye on them chickens while I was doing my chores and for the life of me I couldn't see anything really wrong. Then one morning I happened into the barn a bit early and looked into the chicken coop and not a chicken was in it. I looked outside and eventually I found them all huddled up in one corner of a

field. Well I corralled them and got them back into their pen where I fed them. They seemed happy enough when I threw down some feed for them to eat, so I left. The next morning I got up and as I walked into the barn I seen the chickens were all out of there pen again and no where to be seen. I headed on out to the field and sure enough I found them in the same spot as the last time, all huddled up in one corner of the field. This time though out front of the old hens was the rooster and he had his back in the air and looked as if he was warning something to stay clear. In other words he was protecting all the hens.

So I decided on leaving them for a bit and hid myself behind the stone fence, so I could see them, without them seeing me. For about an hour nothing happened and I kind of dosed off a bit, until I heard the old Rooster just a cackling and making a heck of a ruckus. I looked up and low and behold there in front of the rooster with his teeth bared was a big old red fox. I got up an chased him away and went and got Reg.

"Well," said Reg, "looks to me like you found out the problem why them hens aren't laying the eggs they used to. That there mangy old fox kept scaring them out of their pen." Looking a bit closer at things later on we found that that fox had dug a hole up under the back of one wall letting him right into the pen itself.

"The rooster by the looks of it George, has been fighting off the old fox and so far has been doing a good job of it too, as we didn't loose any.

"Yep that would be it," I said, "looks like our problem is solved other than getting rid of the fox."

"I will look after that," Reg said, and, well he did."

After that the hens got back to laying and Reg never missed another morning without his eggs and bacon. As Laura would always say. "Nothing worse than starting out the day with a grumpy old farmer."

For most parts things like that happened and when it did, one had to just sit back sometimes and let the problem come to them, so they could fix them.

In todays world folks are so busy with making money and paying bills, they don't take the time to slow down when problems strike. For me and my wife though living here in the country, I have found that in the last few years that slowing down has been the answer to over half of our problems now in life. Guess you might say, one should take the time to breath in a bit more of our fresh northern air and in doing so....things will work out.

Days With Jennie

You know....for years growing up, there was never a day that I didn't take my horse Jennie out for a ride. I know I enjoyed it and I am sure she did too, seemed as soon as I walked into the barn she would stamp her foot just itching to get out. I gotta' say she sure was a frisky one and when she got to running, run she did, that tail would be standing straight out.

There was something special about that horse, she had a way about her that would just melt my heart. When I was around her close up, she would bend down and put her head over my shoulder, guess you could kind of call it a hug.

One summer about a year after I got her I decided to get to teaching her some tricks, along with some chores which I thought would be beneficial to me every now and then. Like opening doors and carrying my milk pail, from the barn to the house once the milking was done with.

Pulling a small buggy was another but I have to say that just came natural to her, seemed like she looked forward to it every Sunday, as that is when she took Laura to the meeting hall. Thinking about that, seemed every Sunday morning she would walk right over to the buggy and wait for me to hitch her up.

There came a time in my life though, that I began to wonder who was teaching who. One of the biggest, was taking me as a young boy

and helping me to relax, showing me patience and how to enjoy life.

For example, the rides we use to take back through the bush, there Jennie would pick the trails and in doing so, every time I was led to see new and interesting things. If she spotted or smelled a wolf, bear, or deer, she would come to a halt and kind of swing her head in the direction of where the critter was standing or hiding, then wait for me to acknowledge that I had seen it. Sometimes it took a bit of doing too.

One of my favorite places was a secluded place up on a hill looking down on a meadow. Had a nice big old oak tree right on top, with a limb that sort of hung out, just the right height for me to step onto right off Jennies back. Some days I would lay there on that limb for hours just lookin' down across the meadow, while Jennie cropped on the fresh green grass.

One day I remember I had brought some carrots with me for a snack and was laying there chewing on one. Jennie I guess kind of figured she was being left out, so she walked over and put her big old nose up to my face for a bite of her own. I held the carrot in my mouth and you know that crazy old girl just chewed it right down till her nose touched mine, then stopped. For years after that we had a thing when we got to eating carrots. You know? If you haven't felt the softness of a horses nose on your face, you are sure missing out on one of life's most greatest moments.

Also the way she would breath on you, just did something to my insides, as when she did that I just had to give her a big old hug in return.

Yes, I sure enjoyed them days with Jennie as you can tell. Seems there isn't a day that goes by that I don't think of her. Many a times I have told my lovely wife that if we had the money, a new barn would be built out back and 'Jennie Two' would be in the making.

I know you are all saying I am maybe too old for such things any more and should stick to my memories. Well....maybe your right, but when them warm southerly breezes start to blow and my mind gets to thinking, it's as if she is still there for me, giving me that helping nudge.

Helpful Hints-To Remove Coffee Stains. Mix the yoke of an egg with a little water that is slightly warm and use it on the stain like soap. If the stains have been on for some time a little alcohol should be added to the egg and water.

Friend Of A Boy

It was a warm day and as I headed down the lane-way from the barn to the house, I got the urge to go fishing. I went in and assured Laura the chores had been done and where I was going. She never ever minded or said anything about what I did, as long as the work was done and she knew where I was going. I reached up over the doorway in the back porch and took down my fishing pole. Was home made, from a piece of willow, that Reg had cut for me last summer. Caught a lot of fish with that pole.

Pole over my shoulder, I headed on down to the creek which was about a mile or two from the farm. It was pretty easy going on the way down, as it was all down hill, but on the way back, well, I didn't like thinking about that part till it came time.

As I walked along I spotted this big old yeller dog. He made sure of keeping pretty well hid from site, but I knew he was there. I had seen him on different occasions over the past couple months, but never really thought anything about it. Just for a second or two it seemed and then he was gone. Seemed like he wanted to make friends but was just too nervous about doing so.

A short time later I arrived at the old wooden bridge that the creek ran under and went down to my favorite spot, which was on a huge rock that backed up to the bottom of the bridge. The sun always shone on the rock making it nice and warm.

Once settled I threw my line in the water, with a big old worm that I dug up in the fields before leaving home. I then put the one end of my pole up on a rock and a smaller rock on top to hold it from being pulled in the water, in the event that I caught one. I then settled back to just soak in the day, and a beautiful day it was.

With the rock being so warm and with the breeze blowing over the water and onto my face, I soon drifted off into dream land. I must have slept for an hour, when the rattling from my pole woke me, and sure enough, I had a nice brook trout on line. I brought it in and put it in my pail that I brought just for that occasion. I put a bit of water in it so it would keep the fish fresh and got to thinking, maybe I could go down stream a bit to where there was a small rapids, I might have a bit better luck there, now that I had been awakened.

With that I put my shoes on, picked up my pole and headed off. I found a nice spot to stand on, a rock aways out in the creek and threw in my line. I stood there for a bit, just admiring the way the water ran down through the rocks. One almost would have to be there to appreciate what I was seeing.

I was so wrapped up in just enjoying the day, when a noise from up above on the bridge, threw me off guard and I slipped on a rock. Out I went into the rapids and was being carried down stream. I let go of my pole, but for some reason I was being dragged down under the water and even with my hands free I couldn't get myself to safety. For the first time in my life, I had a fear go through me that scared me into thinking that I was in real trouble.

I was gasping for air and thrashing around when I reached up, and my arms went around something soft. I realized it was that big yeller dog. He had jumped in and as I held on to him, he took me to the side of the creek and to safety.

I crawled up on the bank and the dog came up beside me. He shook himself off and then sat down. I was so shook up and out of breath I couldn't say a word. I just reached out and put my arm around the old dog and he seemed to know exactly what I was thinking. I had made a friend that day.

He never stayed on the farm with me, but he came back a few times a week, as if he was making sure I was alright. On seeing him, I would sit down quietly and he would come up to me, and for a few minutes he would let me pet him, he then would lick my hand and be off. Strange things like that has happened to me through life, on more than one occasion.

My old Indian friend, Grey Wolf told me, animals were never to be taken lightly and that if I treated them with respect, they would do the same for me.

Knowledge

Did you ever have company drop by without knowledge that they were coming? Sure....I expect that is what happens in most cases in todays world.

Years ago though things were done a bit different. I remember Laura would never go visiting without either sending off a note, or calling first, that is when the phones came into being. Just wasn't heard of making an appearance without letting one know, she always said. I know for ourselves we always try to phone first before we drop by someones place, unless I happen to see them outside not looking too busy.

Today things have changed and folks do things differently, whether that is for the best or not is something I guess one has to settle their own mind on.

Kind of like schools and how they taught our young ones years ago. I know when I went to school it was in a one room school house and the teacher there taught all eight grades. I sure had to give her credit as that lady always had time for us children. I don't think I can remember when she didn't greet us at the door without a smile on her face. Her way of teaching back then was a bit different than today.

One way was when we wrote on the old slate boards we had at our desks, we would write, well for example; a few words, then a picture, then finish it off with more words and pictures all entered on the same line. Think they called it illustrated writing, or something to that effect, so long ago I can't rightly remember.

88

On the math part she would start off the young ones by holding up two apples and asking them how many she had. Later on when she got to explaining quarters of something she would bring in a pie. It sounds simple I know, but it sure made it easy for us to learn and exciting, not to forget that after, we all got to enjoy a piece of her pies.

There were many opportunities available in the one room schoolhouse, situations and opportunities that were both special and valuable. One example was that there was the chance for the younger children to *eavesdrop* on the older ones. Thinking back I noticed that when the teacher was telling something to the older students, that the younger ones would be all ears and listening to what was being said.

I kind of figured that the younger children learned more eavesdropping on the things that were not being taught to them directly. It all boils down to that a lot of times, the older kids taught the younger ones, and the teacher knew this, so it was important that the older kids be taught well.

Yes things were done a bit differently back when that's for sure. Some say one couldn't live in todays world with the education that I had. Not sure really what some mean in saying that, as a lot of us older folks seem to be doing quite well today.

Some say that things didn't cost as much back then compared to today. I just laugh and say, "well back then things might have been cheaper, but money wasn't as plentiful as today either. Also one doesn't have to look so far back and take a look at interest rates, darn I can remember when I was paying 18% on a mortgage."

I kind of figure it's up to each individual to what, "Path You Choose" through life. I also believe that you should choose that path yourself and not be swayed into things that others think is good for you.

Helpful Hints-To Keep Cabbage. Cut them off near the head and carry them to the cellar with leaves on for now. Then break off leaves and pack in a light box with stems upward.
When the box is nearly full cover with loose leaves and put a lid on to keep out any critters like mice and so on. They should be kept in a dry cellar.

Helpful Hints-To Keep Potatoes. They should be kept in a cool dark place. When old and likely to sprout, put them in a basket and lower them for a minute or two into boiling water. Let them dry and put them in sacks. This destroys the germs without injuring the potato and allows it to keep its flavor for a longer period of time.

Music

Over the years I have always admired the folks that could take a musical instrument and make it sing. When I was young the instruments weren't like some of the ones today, not by a long shot. Some were even made by using just a stick of wood.

The first Flute I ever made was out of a dry limb taken from a tree of all things and with the help from Grey Wolf, who lived not too far from us, we brought a beautiful instrument to being.

Grey Wolf, as a supplement to his income, made flutes throughout the summer months and sold them in the southern United States throughout the winter months. I gotta' say, he could sure make them sing.

The nice thing about the old Native American Flute, is that one doesn't really have to be able to read music to play one. With just a bit of showing, one can be playing beautiful music within a half an hour. I guess that's why I have enjoyed them so much throughout my life.

I was very fortunate that old Grey Wolf took the time to teach me his learnings on Flute making and it gives me great pleasure in making them in todays world for folks. I make a lot of them and in over thirty years I have never had a person come back saying, that they haven't enjoyed them. Seems that when one gets to playing their flute, a feeling of contentment and happiness takes over their

thinking. Sure can't be a bad thing in the hectic world like we live in today.

Another couple objects that most carried back then, was jackknives, and mouth organs or harmonicas on the belt. I for one always carried a mouth organ, either on my belt or in my shirt pocket.

Old Reg used to tell me. "Never go out to start a day without your mouth organ George, as you never know when the urge might hit ya." And you know, over the years I have found that to be so true, as many a day when that urge did hit, I would find a nice spot under a shade tree and get to striking up a tune or two.

Seemed that when my mind got to wandering off onto things that it shouldn't, a song or two would get things back to their right perspective.

The guitar was another musical instrument that was used quite often and it seemed to me that no matter where or when, it too always sounded good. The nice thing about the old guitar was you could sing along while strumming it, as with a mouth organ you couldn't.

Many a nights up the road aways at Horace & Nancy's, *Reg and Laura's daughters place*, the old guitar would be brought out. When Horace got to playing and singing, well let me tell you, if there was a time in my life that I never wanted to end, this was it.

Nancy and Horace always treated me good, and when in their midst the feeling that came over me, well, it's hard to put into words. I guess you could say it was a home feeling, yes that would be it. A warm place, were one would feel loved and wanted. Horace is gone now in part, but in my mind I can still see his friendly smile when walking into the room, that can never be taken away.

Nancy is still with us. I do see her occasionally, which in all sincerity should be more. She is a one of a kind lady, as her mother and the love that she has shown me over the years while growing up, again, can never be lost. You just have to love her.

Back to the guitar playing, you know I always wanted to be able to play a few notes but just never found anyone to give me a few lessons. They say though your never too old to learn, so....maybe one of these days I might just give it a try.

The thing about the instruments I grew up with was that they didn't need a whole band to make beautiful music, one person if they had a mind to could do it all on their own. Takes a special person I always figured that had the talent to bring folks alive, or to tears for that matter. I could never get enough of them throughout my life and if there was something that I could wish for; it would be to have my old friends back, sitting around the stove singing up a storm, with Laura and Nancy fixing up a nice hot chocolate for us all.

Television
Today & Yesterday

You know taking a look at my life as to how things have changed throughout my years, well....lets just say its been quite a ride.

One item that I am sure everyone would say was a big ticket item, was the television set. For most of my early days I never got to see a TV as they were not readily available to everyone. Another reason was we were just too busy to watch it, even if we would have had the luxury of owning one.

My only TV with a screen was looking outside through a window from our kitchen or bedroom. Have to say I still enjoy looking out, especially where we live now, as there isn't one window that hasn't a fantastic view.

I can still remember sittin' at my small desk in my bedroom many years ago, looking out the window, letting my mind make up things Sometimes I would plan my whole life.

The old rooster on the fence was sure a sight to see and for many an hour I sat there watching him trying to figure out what was going through his mind.

The cows lazing around the pasture was another site to see and again many hours were spent just watching them swatting flies with their tails. Relaxing, if nothing else.

The geese every fall would fly right past my window, seemed they knew I was watching and wanted to fly by and say, "see you next

spring my friend." I would wave with sorrow in my heart knowing they wouldn't be seen again for many a month.

My horse Jennie would be my most favorite show, as I just couldn't get enough of her beauty, as to how her gold coat would shine in the afternoon sun. Sometimes she would glance up at me with a look that seemed to be saying. "I am waiting, come down and lets go for a ride."

Each and every morning I couldn't wait to get out of bed, look out my window and see what new was waiting to greet me. Might say it gave me a reason to get out of bed.

Our first TV came one Christmas, as Laura felt it was time we caught up with the neighbours, that lived in the big city. Not that Laura was the kind of woman that felt she had to do these things, but, well to be honest, I am not sure what her thinking was on the subject.

At any rate we did get a TV some years after I moved in with them. Black and white of course, as there was no such thing as color. When color did come out I can still hear Reg saying. "You know I can't ever see a TV like that going any place, folks just won't want it." Of course now one has to remember that the colors back then sure weren't like today, let me tell ya. Looked awful in some respects, but none the less it was color.

Even after the TV did come into our home I didn't get to watch it much, as I was usually too tired and headed off to bed. Reg did get to enjoying boxing every Sunday night and I can still see smoke rolling out of his old pipe when he got excited. Kind of looked like one of them old steam engines you seen coming up to the railway depot, smoke just a flying with the train whistle howling away. Sure was a site to see that's for sure, think I enjoyed watching him more than the boxing.

One thing was for certain, even though Laura was the one that brought the TV into our home I never once seen her sit down and take in a show. Oh I guess she listened to it while working in the kitchen, as my wife does today, but I never seen her really sit down and really watch a whole show.

Some nights being so cold it took a good five minutes or so for the TV to warm up before we were able to watch it. Then when the fussy screen came into view we all sort of held our breath, as we never really knew what we were going to see, as TV guides right then were unheard of.

As the years flew by new television's were put on the market, color sets that Reg said would never sell were selling by the millions. Antennas were upgraded eventually that would reach around the world and I would have to say not many a home was without one.

Today they are so slim and trim that they fit anywhere and compared to years ago are sure a sight to see. Yes the old TV has

come a long way that's for sure. But....if asked what was the nicest TV I have ever owned. I would have to say, that the TV's of today, couldn't hold a candle to that small window that sat above my desk in my bedroom, many years ago.

As today I can still visualize the shows that came to view every day and night of the week.

Helpful Hints-To Clean Tobacco Pipes. Pour alcohol into the bowl and allow it to run out the stem. This will thoroughly clean and sweeten the pipe.

Helpful Hints-To Measure Hay. Fifteen to eighteen cubic yards well settled in mows or stacks make a ton; 20 to 25 cubic yards make a ton when loaded on a wagon from mow or stack; 25 cubic yards of dry clover make a ton. To find the number of tons in a mow multiply the length, width and height in yards and divide by 15 if well settled and by 18 if not so well settled.

The Common Cold

Catching a cold, now there is something most folks don't like to hear about or catch for that matter. Colds have been around us humans from day one and probably will be around long after we are gone too. Now a days they tell us colds can't be caught by going out into the cold, wet feet doesn't give you a cold and a whole mess of other things. Well I am no doctor by no means and don't pretend to be. But I have my own feelings on this cold thing and I thought I would share them with you.

For years on the farm and going to the old one room school house five days a week, in all kinds of weather, colds were hardly ever heard of. We had over fifty young ones in that school and not very often was a child home sick with a cold. I got to thinking about that and here is what I came up with.

For most of my younger days, Laura and Reg in the winter time would make sure when I went out, that I was dressed properly. The main thing they told me was to keep my feet dry and warm, along with my head and neck covered. I still am a firm believer that you can catch a cold, by getting cold and not dressing properly. I believe we all carry a few bugs in us and our body for most parts can keep them at

bay. But if we get too cold, or over tired, our bodies go on to trying to fix them problems, leaving the door open for the bugs to take hold.

I also was taught from day one, to wash my hands after using the wash room, or going out in public. The main thing, if I couldn't get to a place to wash my hands, I was to never and I mean never, to touch my face with my hands. Over the years I made that into a habit and even today I try to never touch my face. It's hard in today's world though, as there is so many different kinds of bugs out there. Most have been brought over to us by other countries and not much we can really do about that part.

My family and I though, have taken precautions like I mentioned above and we hardly ever catch a cold or get the flu. The flu is another thing that is over rated in my books. We don't get the flu shot, as we have a bad feeling about it. I kind of think that we will pay some day by us playing with these flu shots and using all this antibiotic soap. We never use it in our house and won't use it. I believe that all they do is make the bugs more resistant. Just good old hand soap is what we use and over the years it has kept us all safe. We raised two fine boys and they hardly ever caught a cold growing up, living at home. One time though, I caught a cold while visiting my sons, at that time he lived in a basement apartment and the owner had strep throat and I picked it up there, along with my son too.

My wife fixed it though, by getting me to drinking tea we make from the Linden tree out back of our house. The old saying though about catching a cold is so true. Two weeks a coming and two weeks a going. I had an old doctor friend and he said. "Well George, I can give you some medicine and it will take a couple weeks for the cold to go away, or you can let it run its course, and it will be gone in about two weeks. He is right too.

I also am a firm believer in staying out of any hospitals or doctors offices, unless its absolutely necessary, them places can make a fellow sick. I get some blood work done every few years or so, but other than that, I leave my body alone and I got to admit, I know it pretty well.

My wife is the same and over the years we have come to know, if something just isn't right inside us. That's the nice thing in life, we are given free will. Well in most things, as the powers that be in this country, like to think they run us. What I do there is, just let them think what they like and go about and do what I want. Been working for us for the past fifty some years.

So there it is, a bit about the way I feel things should be done and if you really look, I think you will find that over 75% of old Mom and Dads advice and remedies worked. Also, a lot of them are being brought back and used in todays world. Makes you think doesn't it?

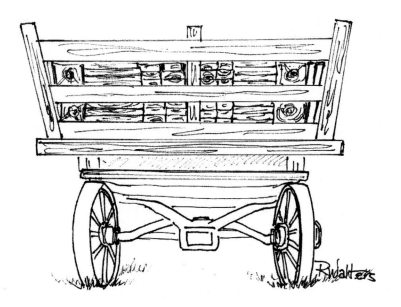

The Cottage

"**T**he Clyde's are hooked up over by the barn there George having a drink. Once they get their fill bring them on over here to the house and hook them up to the hay-wagon. We have to go and pick up a load of lumber at Jim's place, as I would like to get to building that cottage on the lake."

I didn't mind as I just loved going to the lake through the summer months, as it gave me some time to do some serious fishing and boating.

Once over at the house, Laura had a hot chocolate waiting for me and a sandwich. I have to tell you that lady sure could make good hot chocolate, just made my mouth water thinking about it. My sister Barb many years ago made it especially good too though.

"I thought that things were a little tight this year for money Reg? I asked. "Do you think we can afford to buy the material to build that cottage?"

"Well," said Reg, "it's got to be done sooner or later and the way things are going on around the lake these days I think we had better get at it. It won't strap us too hard, as I made old Jim *the fellow at the mill,* a trade for most of the lumber. He needed hay and I needed lumber, so it worked out real well."

"Well I for one think it is a great idea," said Laura, "as you two fellers have been loafing around here far too long anyways, for the past two weeks. Think just because the haying is all done and other things caught up you can just sit on the front porch giving me orders? Well let me tell you."

With that Reg took hold of my arm and said, "lets get out of here before she gets to hollering. We don't need the neighbors up the road thinking we are having a fight or something."

"Hollering? Who do you think you are? What do you mean? I don't holler. I just speak the truth."

With that I grabbed my second half of my sandwich, gulped down my hot chocolate and we were off. Looking back I could see a smile on Laura's face, so I knew then she wasn't really serious. She was just funning with old Reg. She did that quite a bit now that I think about it. I liked to believe it was her way of getting us out of her hair, along with letting Reg know it's OK to be taking time off from all the daily chores and farm life, once in awhile.

Up the road we went, me taking the reigns as I sure enjoyed driving the team of Clyde's. Not that it was much to it, as I mostly just sat there and enjoyed the ride, along with Reg's company. It wasn't too far up the road, maybe three miles or so and that gave Reg and me some time to chat, which mostly was tales of his younger days. Along with them stories that he would bring to being and smelling his old pipe, I figured I was about the luckiest young feller in the world. Seemed like no time and we were at Jim's.

Reg he got off and got to talking to Jim while I stayed on the wagon, as the two old Clyde's for some reason just didn't like the noise the saws were making in the mill. Guess not being around them too often kind of spooked them a bit. So I talked quietly to them, letting them know that things were OK..

"Bring that rig of yours over to the barn there George, where that lumber is piled. You can see it there right beside the well. That's your lumber, got it all cut and piled there for you a few months ago. Been drying there on stickers, so should be some real nice stuff."

I flicked the reigns and away we went. It never ceased to amaze me how them two old horse knew their job. They pulled the old wagon right over to the pile of lumber as if they knew exactly what Jim had said.

I climbed down and before my feet hit the ground lumber was being piled onto the old hay wagon. I was just about to grab a board and help out when Jim said. "George; Sara is in the house over there and I think she has just finished up making a fresh apple pie. How about you going and getting yourself a piece and a couple more for

Reg and myself. Won't take us long to load this, no offense, but every so often a job can have too many hands."

"I understand," I said, and away I went over to the house.

I walked up onto the porch and sure enough looking in through the screen door I could see Sara busy taking the pies out of the oven.

"Hope I am not bothering you Mam, just that your husband said to come on over, and well, he said."

"I know, he said that I am making some pies and to give you a piece, am I right?"

""Yes Mam, I sure would like a piece, oh and he said to do up two more pieces for him and Reg, if that's OK with you Mam.?"

"Just fine George, come on in here for a minute and chat for a bit. Them fellows out there won't be done loading that wagon for a piece anyways." With that I opened the door, went in and sat down at the table.

"Here is a piece for you while we are chatting." With that she took about half a pie and laid it on a plate in front of me.

"So how is Laura doing these days? Is that man of hers lookin' after her and treating her good? You know you can tell me if he isn't."

"Oh no Mam, Reg always treats her good, you know that."

"Yes I know, there isn't a better man than old Reg."

"What about Jim your husband? Isn't he a good feller?"

Looking at me, she smiled and said, "now don't you go off running and tellin' him this, but I love that old feller more than life itself."

"I won't," I said, "I am good at keeping secrets."

After a bit more chattin' I put my plate in the sink and headed on back to the mill.

"Bout time you got back here, we had this wagon loaded an hour ago," said Reg.

"An hour ago, your just joshing me, I was only gone for maybe a half hour at the most."

"Did that wife of mine talk your ear off? She is good at doing that to young fellers that drop by you know."

"Nope not a bit Mr. Jim, enjoyed every minute of it."

With that we finished up our pie and home we went.

The lumber was then brought up to the lake the next day, which I should say took most of the day. The following day we got into building the cottage.

It is still standing today and for a good number of years, Reg, Laura and myself had some great old times at the cottage, while visiting the lake.

The Gift

It's not the big things in life that matters so much I have found, it's the little things.

I had just gotten out of bed, dressed and went down stairs for breakfast. Laura was cooking up a batch of bacon and eggs, the eggs fresh out of the hen house. I have to say there is sure nothing tastier than farm fresh eggs. Once done I asked if there was anything special that she needed me for and she said, "not this morning. Why? Do you have something in mind?"

"I was thinking of visiting old Grey Wolf, as I have a birthday party coming up for the teacher and Grey Wolf could help me with what I had in mind."

She smiled and said, "good idea, but be back for the evening milking and don't forget to let Grey Wolf know I said hi."

"Will do." I said. With that off I went and in a half hour or so I was back at Grey Wolf's cabin. Today he was sitting on his porch whittling something out of wood. I asked him what it was and he said, "what ever it ends up being." Well, couldn't argue with that I though.

"So what brings you here today young one," he asked?

"Tomorrow we are having a birthday party for the teacher and I just know everyone is going to bring her something. Thing is, I don't

have any money to buy anything nice and was wondering if you had any ideas."

"The teacher stays in a house just up the road from you, doesn't she?"

"Yep only a stone throw away," I said.

"First of all tell me a few things about this lady, as it will help me in figuring out what she might like."

"Well, she is a good teacher and dresses pretty good. She likes apples and all kinds of things that are simple it seems. She even likes snakes and critters, although I think she likes birds the best, as she is always telling us something about them."

"Hmm, said Grey Wolf, that gives me an idea. If she likes birds so much, maybe she would like a bird house."

"Ya that would be a nice gift for sure. But I don't have any wood or nails to build one and actually I don't even know how to go about making one."

"You don't? It doesn't take much in the way of things to make a birdhouse and if you look real hard, you can make one for free, lets go for a walk."

With that we got down off the porch and headed on out to the bush. Once back in aways he asked, "look around young one, do you see any birdhouses out here that you could use?"

I looked at him and said. "Here in the middle of the bush? Nope don't see a one."

"Your not looking too hard then. Where do you think the birds live? They live all around us and here is where they make their homes. Take that tree over there that is broken off. Look at the hole on the one side of it. I bet inside the tree, it's hollow. What a nice spot for a home wouldn't you say?"

"Never thought of it that way," I replied.

"Thing now is, we just need to find an old log that is hollow and not being used."

That was no problem and in a few minutes we found over a dozen. After looking them over we picked a nice one and broke off a piece near the bottom about a foot long. We took it back to his cabin and on the way in, he grabbed a piece of old sheet metal that was laying up against a lean-too. He broke off a piece and we fastened it on the top of the log for a roof. On the bottom we fastened on a piece of thick bark, and we had ourselves a bird house.

I couldn't believe how nice it looked. "Do you think she will like it?" I asked.

"You bet she will, said Grey Wolf, "you wait and see."

Well I thanked him and headed on home.

You know when it came time for her party, out of all the gifts that she had given to her, she liked mine the best. For years it hung just outside her window and every spring she said it had at least four families come an go.

When she left our school she brought it over to me to keep for her, which I did as she was moving to the city.

"This belongs here in the country," she said, "and I want you to take good care of it."

I hung it on an apple tree just outside our kitchen window after that and as far as I know it's still there.

So there you have it, a simple thing that didn't cost a cent, but meant a lot to one country school teacher.

Helpful Hints-Eye Wash. Sore and inflamed eyes may be cured and strengthened by frequently bathing them with salt water.

Helpful Hints-Strawberry Worms. Chickens will destroy them. They should be turned into the patch before the berries are formed.

Helpful Hints-Corn Moths. Fill up all the cracks and sweep the floor and walls clean before storing the corn. To destroy the moths, fill all cracks then sprinkle the floor with a mixture of strong white wine vinegar and salt before laying up the corn. If the moth has deposited its eggs on the grain salt may be mixed with it.

The Golden Rules

Over the years I have written many a story about the folks that raised me along with others that shared their wisdom. These folks with different techniques, mostly from their upbringing made me what I am today.

Years ago folks had a rule of thumb to go by, which some called, *The Golden Rules.* There isn't too many folks today being taught it in schools I am sure, but for us older folks, well....nothing was more important.

So for those that hasn't learned the Golden Rules let me enlighten you some.

The first One was very important which read;

"*If you open it close it.*" Now that might not seem too important to some folks and some would even say; "What could I possibly learn by doing that?"

Well, lots can be learned, as you can save yourself a lot of grief by remembering it. For example; what would happen if you had dairy cattle and left the gate open that led out into the wild or onto a road? Nothing good that's for sure. What would happen if you left the barn door open leading to the hay mow in a storm? You might just loose your roof, that's what.

What would happened if you left the door open in your home? Loss of heat, flies all over everything, well just too many to name. So

you see it is important to always keep it in the back of your mind that whenever you are at home, or at a friends home, if you open it, close it.

Two....***If you turn it on, turn it off***. Simple as it might sound lots of folks don't do it and wonder why they are in debt. Some examples would be the light switch, if your not in the room why have it on. If your working around equipment turn it off before you start fixing anything, or...if your done with it. There are many, but if one keeps the golden rule in mind, you never know, it might save your life or a friends life some day.

Three....***If you unlock it, lock it***. Like your house door when going out for a visit, your car when going into a shopping mall, at least now a days, or your most favorite diary, so no one can read what you have written, just to name a few.

Four....***If you break it, repair it***. As you will be needing it in the near future and nothing worse than having to take time from a busy day to fix something, that should or could have been fixed when it happened.

Five....***If you can't fix it, find someone that can fix it and get it done***. Especially if what you broke wasn't yours.

Six....***If you borrow it, return it***. As there is nothing worse than someone borrowing something and having to go and ask for it back. Over the years lots of folks stop loaning things just for that reason.

Seven....***If you use it, take good care of it***. As you wouldn't want someone to borrow something of yours and run it into the ground and then return it to you not worthy of anything anymore.

Eight....One that took me awhile to do and still can hear Laura saying;

"George, ***If you make a mess, clean it up***. As it sure makes it easier for others around you." I did learn to do just that and it has helped not only others but myself too. Although my wife today calls them happy trails.

Nine....this one is quite special to me. ***If you move it, put it back***. Example would be, I have all kinds of items in my shop that has a spot of their own. When needed I know exactly where to go to get them, saves time and time saves money. My wife and I am sure other women too are the same, having all kinds of things in drawers, desks, dressers you name it, knowing right where things are if needed at any given time. So remember, for yourself or when at others, if you move it...put it back.

Ten....This one is special too. ***If it belongs to someone else and you want to use it, ask permission***. Many a time things have been borrowed without permission, letting the blame fall on

those that were innocent. Not a good thing to do, just ask, saves a lot of grief for you and others.

Eleven....One important one we had on the farm, was. *If you can't operate it, leave it alone*. Many a time folks that have never driven machinery get onto a machine thinking it's fun stuff and end up critically injured or killed. So, leave them alone.

Twelve....*If it doesn't concern you, don't mess around with it*. I have found it has saved me tons of problems by not getting' into other folks affairs. Did it all my life and will keep on doing it.

Thirteen....my lucky number. *If your ever in doubt, ask*. So many problems could and would be solved if one would just ask. My Dad used to say; *"There is no such thing as a dumb question, that's how folks learn."*

There you go, the Golden Rules that use to be taught in our schools, at home and even in the fields while working. Rules to live by that make ones life easier. Too bad they weren't being put into practice more so today.

It was a gentle way of learning, remembering and showing.

Helpful Hints-Sprains And Swellings. Sprains may be relieved and swellings reduced by bathing with salt water. Ointments can be made from the Comfrey plant, which then can be used to treat wounds and reduce the inflammation associated with sprains and broken bones. The roots and leaves contain allantoin, a substance that helps new skin cells grow, along with other substances that reduce inflammation and keep skin healthy. Comfrey ointments were often applied to the surface of the skin to heal bruises as well as pulled muscles and ligaments, fractures, sprains, strains, and osteoarthritis.

Comfrey Recipe-You will need equal parts of Comfrey leaves or roots, *roots is more stronger,* olive oil, and melted beeswax. Chop Comfrey leaves or dried roots and add to olive oil. Warm over low heat, but do not allow mixture to boil. Cover and let stand for 24 hours. Strain then add melted beeswax. Apply when needed.

The Old Brown Coat

The coat hanging on the old peg by the door with the Stetson hanging on top wouldn't probably mean too much to some folks with out a little clarification. But thinking back to my farm days, it was a memory that I seen every day, when heading out to do my chores. As that was where Reg would hang his coat and hat. Them two got used a lot, let me tell ya.

Simple things like that brings back lots of memories, could say fond ones too. The reason though the old coat hanging by the door was something special was; that the days back when weren't always rosy as some would like you to believe, there was some real hard times.

Hard times back then meant not having food enough to eat for the cold winters or not enough firewood to heat ones home, things like that. We did OK though, as we grew most of our own food, as most folks did in and around our area, but there was a few that didn't.

Like the lady down the road aways, she was a lady of means and had lived a hard life. Her husband was the sort of feller that if he made any money throughout the year, it would burn a hole in his pocket, till he had it all lost in a poker game, or spent it on, some good tasting corn mash cut to not less than 40 percent alcohol, or so they told me.

When winter hit he would head on to different towns to work, or so he said and leave his wife to fend for herself. Laura and Reg would do what they could to help the lady, but she was a lady with her own

mind and didn't take too kindly of taking charity or things of that sort. In other words, she was a proud woman which in Laura's eyes was the way a woman should be.

Well the time came one year that her husband didn't return from town. Later we found he had been shot and killed in a brawl at some hotel. Folks did what they could for the lady, but for most parts she was left alone.

I got to feeling bad for her and came up with a plan that would let me help her without her thinking it was charity; and decided right there and then to put this plan into motion. I saddled up Jennie and headed on over to her place and as I rode in the lane-way I could see her in the kitchen working over the stove, with a wool shawl wrapped around her shoulders.

I got off Jennie, tied her up to the front porch railing and knocked on the door. To my astonishment she welcomed me with open arms. After the hugging was done with, she asked what brought me.

"Well," I said, "I heard in town that you made some coats and things for folks?"

"Yes I do, why do you ask?"

"Well I was thinking, that Reg is in need for a good warm coat as you probably know and I kind of figured maybe we could make some kind of a deal."

"What deal would that be George?"

"Well I was thinking, if you would make the coat for Reg out of some hides that Laura has up in her chest, that I could do some work here on the farm for you as payment. I know it isn't cash but I am a good hard worker and I guarantee I will make it worth your while."

She looked at me for a minute and said. "You sure your not just doing this because your feeling sorry for me? As if you are I won't be having you around my place for one minute longer?"

"No Mam I would never do that. I just know that Reg is in dire need of a new coat and Laura and me, we figured it would make for a nice Christmas present."

Well to make a long story short, the coat was made and I helped her with the chores and things around the farm for a good many years. She never got cold either, as I had the wood box filled each and every night after school and throughout the summer I fixed the barn, fences and even helped in the spring in getting her garden ready to plant.

Not to say that I didn't get rewarded after the coat was paid for either, as I did, in so many ways that one could not name them all. But the best part was, just seeing that brand new hide coat hanging by the door, on my way out to do my chores each and every day.

The Old Cook Stove

"**G**eorge pick up your gloves there and hang them here by the cook-stove so they will be dry and nice and warm when milking time comes. Hard enough doing your chores without having cold hands." Yep they were the days.

I have always felt that the cook-stoves of years ago was about the most important piece in ones home. Just to name a few of its duties would be, well let me think;

One that I just mentioned about drying things was right up there on the list, but of course the main use of the old wood cook-stove was for cooking and when it came time to cook or bake things there was none better, even by todays standards in my eyes.

Cooking though had a few draw backs, as on the farm what one does or when one eats is never known for certain. If we were out in the fields we usually finished up what we were doing before stopping no matter what time of day. It was hard for Laura not knowing when we were going to be home for dinner or supper, but she took it all in stride.

Around five she would start supper unless it was a roast or chicken, then she would have had it cooking in a pot in the oven for most of the afternoon. If things got cooked before we arrived, the old cook-stove

had a warmer oven on the top where she would set things which kept them warm.

Never a meal did we have that was cold, was unheard of back then, at least with those that had a good wood cook-stove.

I can still remember coming in from a cold winters day, my feet almost blue. Laura would set me down on a chair in front of the cook stove, help me with taking off my boots and then asking me about my day while rubbing my feet. Once she figured the circulation was back she would then hand me a dry pair of socks to put on. Then she would open up the oven door, lay a block of wood on it and there I would rest my feet, till they both were nice and toasty. I have to tell ya, the warmth from the old cook stove could take the worst of cold out of anyones feet.

Many a evening I drifted off to sleep while warming my feet listening to Laura humming her favorite songs while she cooked supper. Never seemed to bother her either with me stuck right there in the way.

I also found another good spot to sit and get warm and that was in the wood box which sat beside the stove and if asked I would have to say it was my most favorite spot. While sitting there I felt safe, kind of like at nights when one hides under the covers, something like that.

The old wood cook-stove was also used for warming up water for doing the dishes, as it had a reservoir on both sides and there was never a time that we didn't have warm water for washing our face or hands. Come to think of it, there was just enough water in them two reservoirs to do the laundry or take a bath. The latter not one of my most favorite things to do.

Another thing I loved about the old wood cook-stove was that the food like meat, fish, pies, cakes or cookies that Laura was cooking or baking at the time, got to mixing with the smell of the wood, well...I have to say that them aromas made my stomach growl and yearn for what was to come at supper time.

In the mornings laying in bed, the aroma of bacon and eggs or pancakes would come drifting up the stairs, as my bedroom was right on top of the kitchen. Let me tell you, it wasn't long after that first sniff that I was out of bed, dressed and settin' at the table with fork in hand. Still can visualize Laura standing there with her flowered apron on.

But whether it was cooking, baking, warming ones hands or feet, taking a bath or doing the dishes, the one thing that I miss today, is the way the old farm houses were laid out. The old wood cook-stove was up against one wall, with a few cupboards, sink along another and the kitchen table in front of an opened window, with white home made curtains blowing in the breeze.

It was a simpler time in life, hard work, long hours, and hardships sometimes too many to count, but when sitting in the kitchen around the old cook-stove, they all seem to be so unimportant and life was brought back to what it should be.

Helpful Hints-Catarrh. Warm salt water snuffed up the nose several times a day is a simple remedy but one of the best for catarrh. ½ to 1 teaspoon of salt. Pinch of baking soda (to prevent burning – can increase the amount as needed)
1 cup of warm water (filtered or previously boiled water)

Helpful Hints-Bean Soup. Boil one quart of beans till soft, then rub through a colander to remove hulls. Return soup to the stove, season well with pepper and salt, and add a few spoonfuls of cream; serve with small squares of toast. Some prefer corn bread with bean soup. If desired some bacon may be boiled with the beans, as it adds richness and flavor to the soup.

The Old Milk Cans

One time while out driving around I spotted an old milk can sitting on a veranda of some ones home. They sure had it painted up pretty, but looking at it kind of made me feel sort of sad. Reason being I suppose, as back on the dairy farm the old cream cans were an everyday item, one might say they were on top of the list back then.

If it wasn't for them old cream cans, a lot of farmers wouldn't be where they are today. I remember each and every morning the milk and cream cans would be picked up and other cans dropped off. Laura use to leave them on the front porch on the cool days and move them around into the shed on the hot or warm days.

As soon as the truck left in the morning she would take the cans and make sure they were clean inside, which for most parts always were. If not up to her expectations though, she would rinse them out with boiling water that she had in the reservoir of the wood cook-stove and then let them stand to dry. While drying, we would head on off to the barn and get to the milking, which usually took us a couple hours or so twice a day. Myself I actually enjoyed the milking and things, not sure why, but it just gave me a good feeling inside.

Once the cows were all milked or should say half milked, I would start carrying the pails of milk to the house. On one side of the old farm house was an addition Reg had build, something like a garage today but ours was mostly used for the milk separator, which was used to separate the cream from the milk. Worked slick that old machine, had a crank on one side and a big stainless steel pot on the top of it. The milk was dumped in the top and as I turned the handle, the cream

would come out one spout and into a pail and the milk would come out another, great invention.

Once we had the cream all separated, we would then take the cream out to the cans that Laura had gotten ready and dump it into them. If they happened to want some of the milk that week, she would fill some other cans too. Not very often they took the milk from us after it had been separated, but once in awhile they would. Made us happy when they did, as we had a few extra dollars that week.

The rest of the milk never went to waste though as we would take what we needed for the house along with some cream and the rest we would carry back to the barn. There it would be fed to the calves or the pigs. The pigs really loved it, let me tell ya, as I would mix it with their chop. Once they got to eating, you could hear them throughout the whole barn, kind of made me hungry listening to them.

Also in the barn, we must have had ten cats and always five or six kittens running around. You know, I never ever figured out where some of them got to. Seemed we always had the same amount at all times. I guess some moved on to other barns around the area. At any rate, I would always put down some of the milk that was left and they sure cleaned it up, think we had the fattest cats around.

About the time I had all the animals fed, the old milk truck would be pulling in the driveway and I would run out to meet it. The old feller driving it always had a few treats on hand for me and I have to say I got to looking forward to him coming every morning. Wasn't much, maybe a sucker or piece of gum, but I never once complained. Myself I preferred gum, as it lasted for a few days, where the suckers were gone in a few minutes. Amazing really how long I could make that gum last, now that I think about it. I had one piece for over a month one time and kept it on the night table by my bed, not sure what ever happened to it, probably Laura threw it out thinking it wasn't any good anymore. Guess young ones wouldn't do that today huh?

Once we got the welcome out of the way, the old feller would load on the milk and cream cans, pay Laura, chat for awhile longer about the weather usually, then drop off some more empty cans and be on his way. Kind of a ritual every morning, but if not for him we would have had to do without a lot of things in life and there would have been some rough times made even tougher.

So there you have it, a bit about the old milk cans and how for some, they just sit and look pretty all painted up, but for me though, a whole lot of fond memories are brought into view, each and every time.

The Old Smoke House

For a good number of years Reg and Laura always had two pigs running around the barnyard. They never ventured off too far, but occasionally I can remember me having to get Jennie *my horse* and bring them on back home from a neighbours field.

Farm animals had a purpose back them, chickens laid eggs and then come fall made nice Sunday dinners. Cows gave milk, and horses did the work of ten men.

I enjoyed each and every one of them, but found it best not to get attached to certain ones; in such a way that was going to cause me a lot of grief, when butchering time came. I know some folks think it is cruel, but one has to remember, that is how we got by back then.

The two pigs now, come fall was done up for meat for winter and I have to say I looked forward to the bacon each and every morning. I didn't get into the not so nice parts of doing them up, as Reg took care of that end of things, which was OK by me.

Once done the pigs were cleaned up over a flame and cut into bacon and ham roasts, along with a bit being ground up into hamburg, as Laura mixed it with our beef as it made things more tasty. It would then all be salted really well and once done it would be hung in our old smoke house. It kind of looked like the old outhouse but around three

times as large and smelled a lot nicer too. Inside the pieces were hung above a smoldering fire which was in the middle of the smoke house on a dirt floor.

Laura looked after that as it had to be done just right, using the right types of wood. Her most favorite was apple or hickory. She would use oak if it was all she had but not very often, old corn cobs were good also. The wood had to be cut a month prior to being burned, as she liked it some green, saying it gave off more smoke. Reg always said you can pretty well use any kind of wood, but one you can't use is pine.

The reason we smoked the pork back then was that pork went bad really fast and being smoked it would last for a long time, that is if done right. Smoking meat back then was an art you might say and Laura never let anyone near the smoke house while she was working.

"Just can't afford to have anything go wrong with the meat," she would say.

The smoke house wasn't anything elaborate, but it was sturdy enough to stop any pesky wolf or wild dog from getting at the meat at night. Along the top by the rafters there was a small pipe just large enough to let some of the smoke out and allow the fire to burn slowly. The meat would be hung in the smoke house till Laura said it was finished.

The meat had to be just right, too hot a fire caused the meat to become soft and if that happened it would just fall off the hooks and be lost, or if it was just left that way it would go rancid and spoil really fast. If the weather was below freezing you had to be careful too, as if the meat froze the smoke couldn't penetrate it and then more problems arose.

If necessary the meat could be left in the smoke house for a couple weeks or so refreshing it with smoke every once in awhile. For most parts we didn't as Laura had a special spot in the ice house.

Today the old smoke houses are pretty well all gone, but back then they were very important, as it was about the only way we could preserve the meat to last through the cold days of winter.

I have to say though my wife and I still love the flavor of smoked meat and come winter we usually have a few smoked hams put away in the freezer.

Helpful Hints-Getting Chickens To Lay Eggs Come Winter. To get eggs in the winter you must make the hens exercise. Do this by keeping the floor well covered with six to twelve inches of clean dry straw, in which you would scatter the morning and evening feed, thus making them work for what they get to eat.

The Salesman

Going to town didn't happen that often on our farm, reason being the trip was around five miles or so. Along with our days being so full ladened down with work, we just plain didn't have the time. We did go though as every farmer did, but only if lucky once a month.

I remember one day Laura was sittin' on the front porch watching Reg work up the vegetable garden just off to one side of the house. Laura was chattin' to Reg while he worked keeping him company as he was her. Don't get me wrong now, Laura did her share of work as she had just finished off helpin' with the milkin', makin' breakfast and had three pies and a pot roast on the go in the oven. Just at that moment she was hot and tired and figured she would get a breath of fresh air.

"Now who could that be?" Laura said.

"Looks like one of those road salesmen. Seems to me we have been getting our share of them lately."

"Well dear they have to make a living too, so we can't be too hard on the feller. Now you just sit there and let me do the negotiating, as if there is one thing I am good at, well this is it."

Laura just shook her head, sat back and watched the feller make his way up to the house. The wagon he had was covered with canvas and inside it was chocked full of all kinds of things. From flour, to magazines, pumps, shovel and axe handles you name it. Behind he was pulling two calves and an old mule.

"What can we do for you?" Asked Reg.

115

"More so what can I do for you?" He replied. "I am sure that a family of your caliber would be in need of some quality items. Am I correct in my thinking my good man?"

"Well depends," said Reg. "As you well know this is hard times and money is scarce."

"Yes Sir I realize that, but one has to remember that I can save you money by not having to go to town. Now take pepper, salt and sugar, I am sure you are in need of them and I can let you have them for much less than they sell it in town."

"What would that be?" Reg asked.

"Sir, I could let you have a ten pound bag of sugar for a dollar, pepper and salt both the same price."

"Hmm, well," said Reg. "That sounds fair to me."

Laura then spoke up and said. "Fair price! I can get it for half that in town. Who are you trying to fool, it won't be us that's for darn sure. At any rate, here is what we need."

"But Laura dear," said Reg, I was just about......"

"Don't Laura dear me, just let me alone here as I know exactly what we are in need of," then looking at the salesman she said. "Write this down, as I am only going to say it once."

"Yes Mam," and with that he took out a pad and pencil."

"Well," said Laura, we need, flour, two axe handles, four good wood milking pails, a new pump for our well, hinges for our fence over there as you can see it hanging. My husband here says it is the reason why it hasn't been fixed. Also in need of some clothes pins and good deep pot for cookin', as mine has a hole in it and I have about patched it for the last time."

I looked over at Laura and she knew exactly what I was thinking.

Oh and some candy sticks for the boy, say around ten or so all different colors. He don't get them too often."

Sure made me happy let me tell ya.

"That is a good order Mam and I am very grateful for your business. Only take me a few minutes here to figure out the cost and will write you up a bill. I only take cash, you realize that, right?"

"Cash," said Laura, "don't you know that us farmers work from daylight to dark trying to make ends meet. Don't you realize that money doesn't grow on trees, or not that I have seen in all my born days."

"Well," said the salesman, "looks like we got a bit of a dilemma here, but I am sure we can come up with something." Looking over at the two geese he said. "Maybe we can make a trade."

Right away Laura had spotted him looking at the geese, thing was we never knew where them two geese came from, they happened in on their own one day while we were feeding the chickens and....kind of

made themselves at home. Laura had said they were too greasy to eat and for most parts they were just left alone.

"Sir I see you are interested in my two geese. We might be able to make a bit of a trade for them. Depends though if your willing to give me what I want for them."

"And what would that be Mam?"

"Well that order that I just told you about for starters."

"Mam, you have to understand that the things you ordered are worth much more than them two geese, fine geese they are, but still you can't expect me to make a deal of that sort."

Laura spoke right up with a twinkle in her eye. "Sir, them are two fine geese, just look at how nice and plump they are. Also you are not just getting two fine geese my friend, you are going to be getting many more, as there is one male and one female and the female is in the family way. Usually they have six or so young ones maybe more. Now if you put them all together, you got, say eight, which is worth much more than the things I asked you for. You have to understand that we have a lot of money and time invested in them two with the feed and all. Actually I never considered parting with them, as they are the finest in the county."

Reg and me scratched our head and looked at the two old geese. I then whispered to Reg.

"Gosh Reg, I didn't know they were so valuable to us."

"Shush now," said Reg.

"Beats me," I thought to my self.

"Well Mam, I never knew that she was in the family way, I would have to take your word on that. But if what you say is true, well then I guess you got yourself a deal."

"Good, said Laura. "Reg you and George go and catch them two geese and put them in a crate for the fellow."

After the salesman left I asked. "Laura doesn't geese lay eggs like chickens? I can't see how she can be in the family way, you just pulled one over on that feller didn't ya?

"Well for one thing, I would never do such a thing, as I have seen the one male making advances toward the female for the past few days now, so I kind of figured we would soon see a few young ones running around here. Thing is we don't need any critters running around here that aren't worth their weight, so figured we should get rid of them. Also I am not sure where they came from anyways."

"Does that mean we sold something that wasn't ours?"

"No it doesn't, as no one I know of in these parts owns geese and we have been feeding them for three months or better, so.. I reckon we can honestly say they were, well, sort of ours."

I looked over at Reg and he just shrugged his shoulders.

"Can't argue with that, dear," Reg said, "but I want you to know I almost had that feller right where I wanted him, and could have gotten a good deal on them things myself without your help."

"Sure you could have and we would have been without money for the rest of the summer."

Reg just lowered his head, knowing fully well Laura was right, and, a lot better at getting things from folks than he was.

At the supper table that night, Reg said. "You know Laura, the next time that salesman happens by maybe you could trade him that mangy old dog that keeps coming around here for a new pair of harnesses for the Clydesdale's."

With that the rest of the night was filled with laughs and life moved forward.

I often wondered how long it took for that road salesman to get his money back from them two old geese, but knowing them salesmen back then, I never had any doubts he would do just that.

Helpful Hints-Plantain Leaves. In case of a bad sting of an insect or snake apply a poultice made of common plantain leaves. This is one of the very best remedies and one does not generally have to look far to find plantain as all are aware who have tried to keep it out of the lawns and gardens. Also very good for mosquito bites stops itch almost immediately.

Three
Generations Of Farming

Years ago things on the farm were sure done differently than today. With my Grandfather and Dads farm, one half of it was bought by my Grandfather years before my Dad got into farming, as he figured he would enjoy growing things. Later on in life his wants changed and he let my Dad have his land to do with as he so chose. When my Dad took over the farm it was in a real bad way. The trees consisted of hundreds of apple, peach, pear and plums which was so let go that anyone other than Dad would have just cut them all down and replanted with new.

Dad though being the man he was got to clearing things up around the bottom of the trees which took all of one year. The second year he got to trimming them down to size which took the better part of that year. The year after that he got to shaping them and the following year he was picking a bit of fruit. Folks dropped by and was simply amazed at what he had done. "All that it takes is work and no-how," he would say.

He didn't just stop there though as while he was getting Grandfathers land back in shape another farm came for sale which hooked onto his. On it was a few good trees with newer varieties; so what he did was he took shoots off the newer varieties and started to graft them onto his old trees. While they got to growing he started to plant all kinds of different trees on his new property.

Within four years he started making some money. It wasn't waisted by no means, and almost every cent was put back into the farm.

I can even remember him pruning and shaping some of his huge old trees real low to the ground leaving them wide. He figured this way it would be easier for him to pick, as he wouldn't need long heavy ladders, and worked great too for a good number of years.

Over the years his work didn't go unrewarded though, as the old trees that he brought back to being put a lot of food on his table, along with a few dollars in his pocket. Which again he put back into his farm or invested it in other land. He never believed in banks, said they were there to make money for themselves not him. I have to say he was right in his thinking too.

When it came to insects bothering his crops he came up with a very unique plan, as back then there was no pesticides like today. I remember one year he was plagued with all kinds of insects and worms in his fruit, so he got to thinking and came up with a program. What he did was, he worked into the soil at the bottom of each tree some old lime, which he had bought up a few years earlier from a hardware store in town that went out of business. He had in his mind that he would stop the insects before they could get to the fruit itself and he was almost right in his first attempt as it stopped over half.

Not being exactly what he wanted he came up with an idea the following year of white washing the trunks of the trees, along with using the lime around the bottoms in the soil. Well for years after that he had fantastic fruit and he wouldn't tell a sole of how he was doing it either. Kind of figured that he had to find it out on his own, so he wasn't about to share it. Well he did later on, but not right then when things were tight with the money coming in.

Grafts that Dad had done on a lot of his trees usually started to produce fruit in three years and as soon as that happened the old trees were cut back leaving the new. I would have to say at any given time some new tree, or some part of an old tree, was always being started.

Gradually pesticides and fungicides were brought in, and farmers from all over started to use them. My Dad did also, as it seemed the thing to do at the time, but he soon found that just after a few short years he started to have more problems than if he had not used the new chemicals at all. So he stopped using them on his trees, but everyone around him didn't. The problem then arose as all the good insects that were needed in keeping the bad insects at bay, was killed off too. End results he was in an awful predicament.

Eventually he decided on buying all the land he could around his farm with the reasoning, that if he owned it no pesticides could be used near his. Within five years he owned land for miles around and

also within that five years his crops started to improve quality wise quite rapidly.

Later on rules and regulations were brought in saying he couldn't sell his pears or apples if they were a touch too small, of if they had a mark or two, or a bit of rust on the skin. He over came this for a few years selling right from his farm and trucking his fruit to market. Then came more rules and they started stopping him from even doing that. He then over came that problem in a small way by throwing half his crop of perfectly good fruit away, only selling the good looking ones. Again it worked for a few years.

I was into it then or should say when all the rules and regulations started and was struggling right along side him. Many a night we would both head off to bed feeling a loss in our hearts, with the women folks almost in tears.

Then by working together we finally got a system going that paid our bills and put food on the table. Was good for a few years till they brought in free trade. Once that happened all our sources that we had to sell our fruit too dried up. Folks started buying from other countries and ours rotted on the trees. We did manage to keep going but eventually other rules and regulations were brought in on where you could sell your fruit and the canning factories started to close their doors. When that happened I decided to sell the farms.

With sadness in my heart we packed our things leaving everything that took three generations to build. Today what was once our farm is mostly houses, pavement and lawns, with here and there a remembrance of an old apple tree that struggles to survive in someones back yard.

I find it hard to put into words my exact feelings of the way farming has gone here in Ontario, but the fond memories of my Dad and me out there in the orchards, are still vividly stored inside my mind.

Yes the orchards are a thing of the past, the old farmers are all but gone, and to add to this, the soil that our energy source has so freely given to us has been destroyed to the point of no return. They call this progress.

Helpful Hints-Soups. Most soups are spoiled by making them in too much of a hurry, and cooking rapidly. Retaining the flavor by slow cooking, and by having a proper soup kettle with a tight fitting cover, is a necessity in making good soup. Have it large enough to contain meat, bones and water and room for skimming. When all is ready an in the pot, place on stove and bring slowly to the boiling point and skim. Now lower the heat and set back on the stove to simmer. Never boil soup as it makes it tasteless and cloudy.

Toilet Seats

Toilet seats, now there is an item that should strike up anyones interest, don't ya think? Well maybe not for some, but for those that are read on.

Years ago back on the farm we didn't have too much of a wash room, especially if you were comparing it with todays. They called it the Outhouse. Did the same job as the ones of today though, just they didn't have a sink to wash up after. But back then things were simple and if one wanted to wash their hands they could just walk over to the hand pump on the well and refresh themselves. But you know, I don't think I ever washed my hands after going to the outhouse and don't recollect me getting sick because of it either. I can see in todays world though, as one is always going into strange washrooms, and one never knows what disease has been brought in by someone before you. So in that case, I guess a sink would be called for, along with a bit of soap.

But back to the toilet seats. In the old outhouse that we had, we didn't even have a lid for the toilet, as it was just a few boards with a hole cut in it. Different size holes were cut for the young ones and later on, slide on lids were developed. Things could get a bit ripe around them places throughout them warm summer days that's for sure.

At any rate due to the hot days, lids were developed which was a good thing. Also took a bit of fear out of a young fellers eyes when trying to get up on to the seat, as it sure looked dark down there.

A few years later the outhouse was taken down and brought into the house, more or less.

"Can never understand why a person would want to have their daily constitutional in ones own home." Reg would say.

"Just don't make sense in my eyes," he would say, "just don't make sense."

But even old Reg changed his way as years past, as I did and everyone else.

Today it's normal to have a separate room in ones house for the bathroom and no one gives it a second thought, amazing how folks ways change huh?

I guess what I liked about it the most was not having to get up in the middle of night, when the weather was around 40 below outside, snowing so hard you couldn't see your hand in front of your face and running to the outhouse.

Now a days we have all sorts of different seats. Some are made of wood, a little hard, but they are what I prefer as I don't make it a thing of sitting there for any longer than needed. But for folks that like to take their newspaper or book to the bathroom, there is softer seats being made, some out of soft foam, some of other things that no one knows.

I have to say now when it comes to the toilet seat of today, they have sure stirred up a few arguments. The biggest thing is that us men don't usually sit to do a number one, so usually the seat is lifted up and yes I will admit, that I forget to put the lid back down every so often. My wife would beg to differ and say I never put it back down and over the years has used different means to train me.

One way was that when she was done with it through the night she would lift the lid and leave it up after she was done, as in the night I usually sat down, as I didn't want to turn the light on. I have to say that sure wakes a fellow up in a hurry reaching for the sides, as with the lid up that hole gets a whole lot bigger. So I do have to admit that us men should pay a bit more attention and after we are finished put the lid back down for our lovely wives.

I hear now they have seats that even play music and ones *that* use technology to take comfort to a new level... and uses just 13 watts of electricity to keep the surface of the *seat* warm at *all* times, boy how times change. Kind of keeps a person imagining what they might come up with next.

So there you go, a bit on old toilet seats from years past, right up and into today. Hmm, I wonder if the wife would like that new fang dangled heated seat for Christmas?

Helpful Hints-Sharpening Knifes. The bottom of most ceramic coffee mugs have a flat, unglazed ring that is the perfect surface for giving that dull knife a quick sharpening. Just run the blade across the bottom of the mug at a 45-degree angle, working from the butt up near the knife's handle to the tip. Slide the blade downward in one direction, keeping your fingers out of the way as you work. Result, no more dull knives.

Washing Machines
Of Old

Another story that comes to mind is about washing clothes. For years my wife and I had an old wringer washer, which I have to say done a darn good job.

After a good number of years of using the old machine I figured that maybe she might like one of those new ones, that did all the work itself, other than taking it out to the clothes line for you. Course in saying that, I would guess that not too many folks even have a clothes line anymore.

Anyways, I sort of thought she would like one of these new units, so one night after we had supper, I said. "How about you and me go and look into a new washing machine?" She looked over at me and said. "Well we sure could use one, as this old one has seen its better day."

So we got things together and headed on out, not too far to go, just down the road aways. Once there we went into the hardware store and I told the clerk what we were after, he said to follow him, which we did. He automatically headed on back to the newer type of machines and started in on telling the wife all about the new features on it.

"I am not too interested in all the new features it has," she said, "all I want to know is how many years would you say a person can get out of this thing and does it do a good job in getting the clothes clean?"

Well he looked at her for a minute or two, as if trying to figure her out and said. "Well, I suppose you would get ten to fifteen good years out of it, if you looked after it and for the cleaning part I would have to say it does a pretty good job."

Well she listened a bit more then said. "You by any chance wouldn't have any new old ringer washers here in the store that I can look at?" Again he just looked at her and finally, I spoke up and said.

"Well you heard the lady do you have one?"

"Well, yes we do, but why would you want one of them, when you can have one of these new machines.?"

The wife spoke right up and said. "For one thing I know they are a good machine, as I have had mine for over twenty years or so, also I know they get the clothes clean, as on the farm we get some pretty dirty fellers. Also for the price difference, I could almost buy two of these wringer ones, for the price of one of your newer models."

So reluctantly, he headed off to the back of the store and again said. "Follow me."

The wife then spotted one almost like the one we had and said,

"Yep, that's the critter we are looking for, put a sold sign on it and we will be back tomorrow with the truck to pick it up." With that we headed on home.

Over the years I have learned not to argue with my wife, as for most parts I found she usually is right; also I know where I get my meals at night from and darn good ones too.

On another note thinking back, I remember Laura use to wash her clothes in an old wash tub, with a scrub board that attached to the one side, she would warm the water up in the wood stove, dump it in the tub, take the clothes and actually scrub them by hand. She did this for years and I have to tell you it wasn't an easy job.

Should mention here though that back then I only had two pair of pants and shirts, I got one change of clothes a week, along with two baths a week. Through the summer I had more, reason being I went swimming.

Later on I was bought a pair of coveralls and before I headed on out to the barn or fields, I would put them on, sure saved on the washing. I will say this though, Laura was a worker and I hardly ever heard her complain, unless us men folks got dirty for no reason, then she would have a few words for us.

Eventually she got herself a new wringer washer and you know, she would still use her old scrub board to get most of the dirt off the

clothes before she put them in her new machine. No need for stain remover back then, her stain remover was her arms.

Yep things were a bit of work back in them days, but we got by and I will say this, that the women in my life growing up were sure something extra special. Today, when I wake up each and every morning, I just can't wait to look at my wife's sweet face.

Helpful Hints-Eating Soup. Soups should not be gulped down or taken into the mouth and then swallowed but held long enough to mix well with the saliva before entering the stomach. One then enjoys what they are eating more and stops stomach upsets.

What Friends Are For

"**Y**ou know your the most pig headed fellow I ever come across Joe."

"What do you mean by that George?"

"Well just the other day up at old Sam's funeral, I noticed you standing way over away from the proceedings. Looked like you were talking to a tombstone. Were you just being antisocial, or did you figure that old Sam wasn't important enough?"

"Well George, I just don't think it's any of your business what I was doing over there. I don't go around asking you a bunch of darn fool questions."

"Well maybe you should."

And with that Joe walked away with disgust.

This story took place years ago when I was just a young feller.

I had made a friend at school one year, a young lad by the name of Joe. He was sort of a quiet fellow but over time, along with a few fights, finding out who was the strongest, we became good friends.

Only thing about Joe, he had a peculiar way of doing things and that just bothered me to no end. Now take me, I was the type of a feller who liked to talk to folks, just enjoyed their company, and when a new one happened by I figured I would take advantage of the situation, but not Joe.

Well as I said, we became good friends and kind of stood up and shared things with each other, was that way for a good many years.

Then one day a strange thing started to happen with Joe, I noticed he was a bit off with the talking part and after school he was more interested in going on home by himself instead of going fishing, like we usually did. I didn't mind at first but after a bit I decided in facing him with it. So one weekend after I got my chores done I rode Jennie over to his place and found him out by the barn.

"Rode all the way over here Joe figuring we might do some fishing?"

"Guess we could," he said, "just hang on till I get my pole and horse saddled."

Well we rode on down to the bridge which was our favorite spot, as under it was nice and cool and on a hot day there wasn't a better place to be found anywhere. Nothing much was said on these days, as well, we both never had much to say and back then company was about the most important part of a fishing trip, not talking. But as I said, I wanted to get this thing out in the open about why he wasn't being so sociable anymore.

"Joe," I asked, "how come you don't want to go fishing anymore after school? You got another friend or something?'

"Well now that you mentioned it, I do George."

"You do?" I asked, *feeling a bit let down*, "and who would that be?"

"Can't say George, just can't say."

"You can't Joe or you won't?"

"Just don't figure it's any of your business, that's all George, nothing personal."

"Nothing personal, not sure what you mean by that, we've been good friends and now all of a sudden you come out with a dumb statement like that."

"Not dumb George," and with that he got up and left.

Well for a few weeks I decided on leaving him alone. Then one day I noticed him riding by on his horse. I didn't call out, as much as I would have liked to but instead I saddled up Jennie and followed him.

I stayed back aways so not to be spotted and to my surprise he rode into the cemetery. I followed him in, got down and tied up Jennie to a tree, which had some nice grass growing around it. I then eased my way down a row of tombstones to find Joe way off in the back kneeling down, talking to someone or something.

I then quietly asked him what he was doing. "Darn George, you near scared the life out of me."

"Well if that has to happen your in the right place Joe. What are you doing here? Talking to yourself?"

"I'm not talking to myself George, I am talking to this Gal that's buried here, her name is Jill Anderson."

"Your what?" I asked.

"Talking to this Gal, you see George, she has been laying here for over fifty years all alone, and well, I just felt sorry for her and decided that if no one else was coming to see her, I would."

"You mean this is who your new friend is, that's why you haven't been going fishing with me after school?"

"Yep that's the reason George, hope your not mad at me or think I have gone off the deep end?"

"Nope nothing of the sort Joe, but do one thing for me, will ya?"

"Sure George and what's that?"

"Well, you go on about your talking to that Gal, but if she starts talking back to ya, I don't want to hear about it?"

"Fine with me George." And with that I left him to his new found friend.

Helpful Hints-Hardboiled Eggs. Eggs boiled for a few minutes only, are usually tough and not easily digested, but if they are boiled for almost an hour they become tender and mealy and are easily digested. If ones stomach is in very bad condition give only the whites at first, then later the yokes may also be given.

I know you are probably saying. "Who in heck is going to cook an egg for over an hour?" Well not many I suppose, but if you were really sick and couldn't hold down food, this is one way to get the nourishment you need, as once the egg is cooked this long it changes things and your body will now except it.

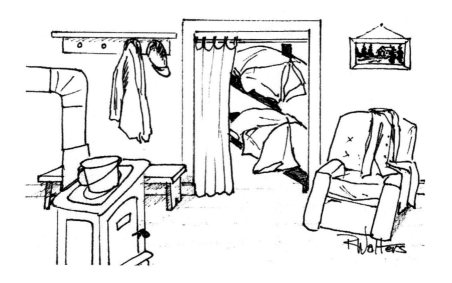

What Makes A Man

Years ago there was one item that pretty well every hunter or farmer got to wearing. They were worn in the winter months, but I have heard certain friends of mine say they wear them year round.

That item would be what we called, long johns, some would say, "I never start a day without puttin' on my longhandles."

Now when you get to talkin' about the old longhandles I have found that in all my days no matter what physique, training or social position one is, there was no hope for any of them to look dignified while wearing them, especially in a hunting camp.

Many a day when hunting with my old buddies, me being the youngest, it was sure a site to see them old fellers walking around at nights in their long johns, let me tell ya. With the rolled up arms and sagging crotch, which looked like a badly put up tent, they would stand around cleaning their rifles, making coffee and swapping stories. Thing was that when wearing these old long johns you have to understand that they hide nothing.

Meaning ones spindly legs, along with bulges here and there; should say they all are right there in the open for all to see. I will say though I never heard too many of the old timers make fun of one another. It was fine though to poke fun at maybe a few extra pounds one had gained from the past year, but that was about the extent of it.

One also didn't send off any stale jokes when one appeared in his long underwear as we knew back then that we all had some flaws.

For myself now I had been watching these fellers and the first year I came up with a plan that I would put on my long johns the first night, then parade around in front of them and get the formality out of the way right off.

Well I did, but it wasn't without a lot of razzing, let me tell ya.

One old feller Howard he got to chattin' one night after the days hunt and being quite diplomatic, said that the old longhandles kept him honest, as at any given time they revealed all his flaws and faults. He then went on to say that no matter whether you are a lawyer, doctor, politician, or minister, all dressed in their fancy daily clothes, that when they got to stripping down to their longhandles, the truth made its presence quite quickly. Made sense to me and made me a longhandle wearer from that day foreword.

Later on as I got older a few of the newer hunters to our group got into wearing some new fang-dangled underwear which came in two parts. The good old back door was gone, along with the hanging and grouping at the crotch and for most parts most of us thought they just didn't look dignified anymore, kind of took the fun out of things. I guess you would have had to live as we did many years ago, to really grasp the full meaning of what it was like to own a pair of longhandles.

One night at the hunting camp that still gets me to laughing was about old Harry. Now Harry, who was our cook, every night after coming in from the hunt, would right away shed his damp clothes and get to cookin' while in his long johns. So one day Dad slipped into his room and got the brand name of his underwear. Later that day he made an excuse he had to go to town for some ammo. Now Harry wore an extra large in size, so what Dad did was buy a boys extra large and brought them home. Back at the camp he washed them and let them dry. Later on when Harry was out visiting the outhouse he took his long johns and replaced them with the new ones he bought.

The next day some real cold weather fell upon us, and I said that being so cold I am thinking that I might sleep in my long johns, and in saying that all the rest of the camp said they were going to do the same.

Later on one by one we got out of our pants and things and were laying around on our cots. Then Harry came out walking funny, mumbling to himself. There in front of us was Harry in his long handles, his sleeves were at his elbows, the bottom of his legs were up around his knees and his crotch was what one would say in a stranglehold.

"Not sure what has happened to them darn longhandles of mine," he said, "they seemed just fine last night."

132

One old feller said, "Harry I am thinking you are eating too much of your own cookin' these days by the looks of it and your gaining weight. Never seen a man grow so much and at seventy years of age too. Got to say I learned something this trip."

With that we all laughed to the extent that some of us had to sit down.

We never did tell Harry what we had done, reason being him being the cook, well lets just say if he had found out, I think we would have went without a few meals or maybe meals that wouldn't be as tasty.

There you go, a tale that lets everyone and everything out into the open, nothing was hid back then, that's for darn sure, why should they be?

Helpful Hints-Maple Sugar Candy. One cup of granulated sugar, one cup of maple syrup, or could use two cups of maple syrup eliminating the one cup of granulated sugar. Then one cup of sweet cream, one half-cup of water and a lump of butter the size of a hickory nut. Boil all together until the liquid will hold together when dropped into cold water. Take from stove and stir until it starts to thicken and then pour into a buttered dish.

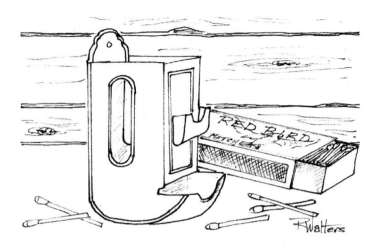

Need A Light

One item that we used a lot years ago, was a small tin match box holder, that held one box of wooden matches. You just opened the box a wee bit, slid it in the holder and at the bottom out would come the matches, readily available. I suppose for most it isn't being used too much these days, but my wife and I have one and use it a lot; as we heat with wood and matches is something one can't be without.

On the topic of matches though, I don't have much use for the ones that are made out of cardboard and come in a package, seems they only work when you don't need them.

Now the old wooden ones, you can strike them pretty well on anything with good results too. I always carry a few in my shirt pocket and if needed they are right where I can get at them. I also use them for tooth picks or something just to chew on. Guess you might say its kind of like one of them soothers that a baby uses. Amazing how certain things just stick with some of us folks, not wanting to part with them.

Another thing I have done, is I take a piece of cloth backed sand paper and take strips off it. I guess they would be around an inch or so wide and about four inches long. One thing about that cloth back sandpaper, you can take it length wise and just rip off a strip. It will come off as slick as a whip and stay straight every time.

I then take the strips and staple them to where ever I might happen to need to light a match, saves on making marks on the kitchen table or walls, so the wife says anyways. I got one in every room and they

sure come in handy especially if the power goes out in a storm and one needs to light a candle or two.

Another use for the old wooden matches was that I found they were real handy for lighting the old lamps that hung from the ceilings. Never had electricity back then and the old lanterns were much needed. One had to be careful with them though, especially in the barn at nights while milking. One mistake could sure make a pack of trouble for a family, but you know, in all the years that we had them, we never had an instance where we had a fire caused by them.

Once in awhile a match might have gotten a bit too close to my finger and made me say a few choice words, but other than that nothing major ever happened.

Also with the old wooden matches they are easy to hold and one is able to reach things easier for lighting, like with them lanterns.

Old Reg he always had a pipe in his mouth and one couldn't ask for anything better to get it going. I remember him calling them, sulfur matches and still can hear him saying. "George, get me a hand full of Lucifer's, can't be without them."

The sulfur smell back then wasn't too good for you to breath and ways of making them changed over the years though, even today every time I light one the memories come floating back to me.

Times have changed though, now a days most folks use throw away lighters. Who would have ever thought that we would be making things today for a few uses then just throw them in the garbage. Was unheard of back in my early days. I for one never owned a lighter that you would just throw away, as I figured they were just a waste of hard earned money. Just give me a few old wooden matches and I would be set for the day.

Now that I think about it, I guess I should go up to the General store soon and get some more, as I am getting a bit low.

Helpful Hints-Flap Jacks. For the best flap jacks you will ever eat, cook up some potatoes and save the water. Then when you get to making them flap jacks use the potato water instead of milk. You will be surprised how good they taste, let me tell ya.

Life Is Freedom

My wife and I have a different outlook on life than most which has done us quite well. In doing so I have had over the years many a folks ask just what that is.

I suppose you could say it has opened the doors of reality and gave us an open mind to do what we want to do in life, in our own way.

I guess you could view my meaning by taking a look at an apple. The seeds in the center of the apple are surrounded by the flesh on the outside; us humans being the seeds, the flesh being an energy, which is our being, or in simpler terms, what we are all made of.

In the beginning we are part of that energy and have the chance of going into human form. Some do, some don't. Once in human form we get to doing what we really want in life, but today I am convinced that our minds are strongly being changed for us before we can do what we really want to do, or for that matter, suppose to do.

I feel that we, as the flesh of the apple, when going into human form, should be allowed to make up our own minds on what we want to do in life. Like our own beliefs and things; we are not allowed to do this, our minds are being changed for us almost the day we are born and the longer we live, the more they are corrupted and the more they are corrupted, the less we do for ourselves; letting in, pain, beliefs that doesn't really set well, diseases, too many to name.

Another example would be the horses of years ago. What the farmer did to train the horses into doing what *they* wanted, I will say this again, what *they* wanted, was *they* put blinders on them. With blinders on the horses they didn't know what was really going on

around them, so in turn, did what the farmer wanted, not what they wanted.

Another way of looking at things is this.

Is what we see really there? Meaning, is what is happening around us really happening? Is the stars for example really there, if no one on earth is really looking at them? Is the sun really warming us, is sickness really able to hurt us, or is it all just an illusion, made up of what we really are? Energy which I call source.

I believe that ones mind, even my own has been changed by others, enabling things to happen that shouldn't be happening, causing the problems that comes to us all. I believe that we are from the very start given the ability to do and believe in what ever we want.

All through my growing up years I have felt that something wasn't just right in what others have said to be true. Something was there gnawing at my insides, making me feel uncomfortable when others got to talking about their views on life. Then one day it was if someone just turned on a light, everything made sense, it all came together and I was content.

As time goes by I believe that the new beings that choose to come here on earth, will learn from the very beginning, of what they should be doing and life here as we now know it, will never be seen again.

Remember this, it's your born given right to your thoughts on life, so choose them wisely.

Helpful Hints-Heartburn, Stomach Ulcers And Good All Round Health. Acidophilus With Bifidus & FOS

Also for Heartburn, frequently allow a few grains of salt to dissolve in the mouth and you will obtain relief from heartburn.

Men & Women
of Yesteryear

Part One

You know some folks get to saying that women and men of today work longer hours and harder than those of, say....the late 1800s and the early 1900s.

Well I am not one to say they are wrong in their thinking, but listening to my old Grandfather one day, talking to a friend of his about a lady back when he was a boy, sure changed my mind on some things.

The story goes like this.

"Mary I am headin' out to see if I can buy us a cow or two over in Little Dixie Landing, should be back in a few days."

"OK Ed but you be careful as I don't think I could handle all this work around here that has to bc done all on my own."

"Don't be frettin' none now, I will be back before you know it, with milk for the table."

"Maybe on your way you could swing by the Grass Widow, wouldn't be too far out of the way, as I have some old clothes you can give her. I don't think she has much in the way of money to buy new things."

Grass Widow back then was the old way of lettin' folks know that Jessica, that was her name, was a divorcee. Her and her husband many years ago where headin' west with a wagon train, she was in

*the family way and when the baby came due they knew they would
have to stop for a bit.*

*Well the others on the train didn't want to wait for them so they
were left to fend for themselves. Which they did, building a cabin by
a small creek surrounded by rich soil. Things went along pretty
good for the two of them but one day another wagon train came by
and her husband hooked up with another woman, leaving her there
at the cabin on her own, with a young baby to look after.*

*Jessica did well for herself and raised that baby to be a fine young
man.*

"Thing is, Ed don't you be staying too long at Jessica's place, don't
want you to be leaving me for another woman like what happened to
her.'

"Now Mary....you know me better than that, after all these years
we've been together and you still don't trust me?"

"I trust you Ed, but not too sure about trusting Jessica."

"Well no matter, don't you get to worrying about that. I have cows
on my mind not women."

With that the next morning Ed was on his way. It would be a hard
trip as half of it was through a piece of desert with no water to speak
of, other than one small hole about half way across.

Mary now knew she had lots of work on her plate with her husband
gone so she set out right away to set up a schedule in her mind for
getting' things done.

The cow they had now was pretty well dried up, but she did manage
a half a pail in the morning and same at night. So first on her list
would be the milking. Once she had that finished up she got to
making butter with half of the milk. Didn't take too long to whip up a
few blocks which would last a week, her being on her own.

Once the butter was done up she got into making bread which
consisted of around five or six loafs. Boy she thought, "they are going
to be right tasty with that fresh butter. Sure hope Ed finds us a good
cow, two would be better, as I kind of think I might be in the family
way. Guess I should have told him before he left, but figured if I did
he wouldn't have left me here on my own and we will be needing more
milk."

Soon as the bread was cooling on the counter she headed on out to
the barn as the animals had to be fed. First was the two pigs which
they raised for winters meat and lamp oil. They also had to have their
pen cleaned out and fresh straw put down.

Then came the chickens which consisted of around twenty along
with an old rooster that gave her a hard time every time she went in to
gather the eggs.

Once done collecting the eggs they would be put in the root cellar which kept them fresh, some feed would be thrown down for them to eat and for just a minute she would stop and watch them, as they gave her a feeling of contentment.

Then the team of horses had to be harnessed up and hooked to the wagon as firewood needed to be brought down from the bush which was about a half a mile from her home. Her husband had it cut and piled but just hadn't had time to haul it in yet.

Along the way she spotted a bunch of buffalo chips which made for excellent burning in her wood stove, so she stopped and picked them up putting them into the wagon. Once done she carried on, noticing the horses snorting and getting nervous. She knew right away it was a pack of wolves that had been in the area so she brought out her rifle from under the seat.

"Don't you two be frettin' none now, I won't let them hurt you."

With just them few words the horses calmed down and carried on their way. Once there, the firewood was piled high on the wagon which took a couple hours or better.

"Going to need to go for a swim in the creek tonight as I am sweating like a horse. No offense now you two, just words. Kind of tired too, so am thinking you two know the way home on your own, so I will rest my eyes a bit."

The wood was brought home and unloaded in a shed by the cabins front door. Some was carried in for the wood stove for cooking and some to take the chill off come night.

For a brief few minutes she made herself a ham sandwich to go with a half a glass of cool milk from the mornings milking.

"Can't drink too much, as I will be needing it for other things later on," she thought.

Milk and sandwich in hand, out to the porch she went and sat down in her old rocking chair.

"Life can't get much better than this," she thought and took her first bite, "Hmm so good."

Once done she unhooked the horses, wiped them down some and put them into the coral with some hay.

"There you go you two, you deserve the rest of the day off, sorry for not getting to you both sooner."

Back at the house out came the wash tub and was set by the well. A bit of hot water was drained from the cookstove mixed with a bit of homemade lye soap. Some more cool water was pumped from the well and also put into the tub. She then went into the cabin and gathered up the dirty clothes her husband had left her, along with her own and some bedding and got busy.

When washed she put them all into an old wooden bushel, carried them to the clothes line and hung them up to dry.

"Good day for drying," she said to herself, "nice breeze and lots of sun, sure do enjoy fresh sheets."

Once the washing was complete some more baking was done and for the time it took her to make the pies she hummed a few of her most favorite songs.

Later on the second milking for the day was taken care of, the team of horses were put into the barn; along with that the cow and the chicken coop door was shut tight, just in case them pesky wolves happened by while she was sleeping.

"Time for a cool bath in the creek," she said, "been lookin' forward to it all day."

Once done she combed out her long hair sittin' on the front porch, wondering where Ed was and what he was thinking at this very moment.

"Better be about me." With that she smiled and went in to sweep out the kitchen and put the pies away, the newly washed clothes were bought in and the sheets were put back on the bed.

"Well Ed, where ever you are, I hope your day went along as well as mine. I am headin' off to bed now, stay safe."

With that off to bed she went, with a feeling of goodness in her heart, knowing she never let one minute go to waste through the day that had just passed.

"Well maybe a minute or two, as I did sit out on the front porch to eat my sandwich. Goodnight Ed." and she drifted off to sleep.

Yep women and men of today have it hard sometimes I grant you that. But for this woman named Mary, well lets just say, she was a.... Temporary California Woman, which means, a woman that is separated from her husband, temporary.

Helpful Hints-Pie Making. In the making of pies, it takes much practice to become perfect. One may have the best recipes in the world and yet fail but the young housewife should not let this discourage her. The secret of pie-making is to use just as little water as possible and get the dough into shape, having everything very cold. Butter or lard should be fresh, sweet and solid.

Men & Women
of Yesteryear

Part Two

Ed said his goodbyes hating to leave Mary with all the chores, knowing she would be a bit lonely, but all in all he knew, she would make out just fine.

It was a warm day and deep down inside the thoughts of riding through a piece of desert wasn't of his most favorite likings, but he knew it had to be done as the old cow they had now was on her last legs.

"Boy fifteen years ago to be exact, Mary and me came to this country, all our possessions fitting into one wagon, pulled by our team of horses and that old cow in tow. Well she has kept us healthy and strong for a good number of years now giving us good milk; so there is no reason for us to complain too much."

The first stop would be at the Grass Widow's, maybe spend a night then head on into Little Dixie Landing. If things go right, should be back home with Mary in a few days.

Would take him the better part of the day to get to Jessica's place with steady riding.

"Well Whiskey Gen," *my horses name*, "not sure what we can get you to eat tonight, kind of depends on what they have on hand. Not to worry though as there is lots of fine green grass around her farm, so

one way or another you will get your well deserved rest, along with a full stomach."

Whiskey Gen came later after we got settled on our farm, guess you could say she was another gift from the land. I was out cuttin' logs for our cabin and here she came walking right up to me, saddle, saddlebag with a few supplies, mostly rifle shells along with a good rope. I figured right off something had happened to her owner, as for most parts a horse doesn't stray too far, unless scared or hungry and in this case lonely.

I talked softy to her and you could tell she was sure happy to see a kind human face. A bit later I swung a leg over the saddle and decided to back track aways to see if I could find who owned her. Sure enough about a mile from where I was working I spotted a feller laying on his side up against a rock. I figured a snake or something had scared the horse and he fell off, striking his head on a rock, breaking his neck. I sure felt bad for the feller but not much I could do for him other than bury him, which I did. Didn't have no shovel to dig a hole but laid him out and covered him the best I could with some rocks for the time being, figuring on coming back later on.

There was no brand on the horse or info on his personal, so only thing we could do was keep her for our own, or until someone else happened by that knew her. Never happened though and we named her Whiskey Gen.

Reason we named her that was one day a whiskey salesman happened by and with a bit of coaxing I got the wife to buy a few bottles, could say just for medicinal purposes or special occasions. Then one night one of them special occasions happened on to us sittin' on our front porch. We had worked hard that day puttin' in seed for our winters hay and corn and decided on celebrating with a taste or two. My wife didn't like the taste much, but she did have a wee bit, probably just to keep me happy. I will say this though, she sure livened up after just one drink. Kind of got me to wondering if we could make this into a reg thing.

Anyways the wife poured me about two fingers in a large cup which I set down on the step. Whiskey Gen was standing along side us at the time as for most parts we just let her roam around on her own through the day, when she wasn't needed. Well Sir, if she didn't walk right up to that glass, tip it over with her nose and lick up the whole thing. She gave a bit of a burp, shook her head and walked away. My wife named her Whiskey Gen, right there on the spot .

As I rode into the yard I could see it had been kept up and in all reality it looked as good as our place.

"Hold up there feller," came a voice from inside the barn. "I got a rifle trained right on your chest there and finger on the trigger."

"Pull in your horns there son, I am not here to hurt or rob anyone, my name is Ed, Ed and Mary, friends of your mothers from way back. You go get her, she will assure you of who I am."

Slowly he came out of the barn into the light where I could see him better, rifle pointing right where he said it was. His mother must have heard all the commotion and came out of the cabin drying her hands with a dishtowel.

She gave me a look over and then said. "Well I'll be darn, if it isn't Ed. How many years has it been? Got to be ten or so."

"Yes Mam, the last time I was here your boy was only a boy, not like the man he is today."

That he is Ed," she said looking over at her son. "He sure has grown some since the last time we talked. Well get down, see Whiskey Gen is still lettin' you ride her?'

"Ya she tolerates me that's for sure, good horse though, wouldn't know what to do without her after all these years."

"James take the mans horse, put her in the barn, give her a rub down and some oats and a half a bail of hay, by the looks of her she has done her share of holding this here fellow up all day. I suspect you haven't stopped since morning?"

"Your right there Jessica, I can still call you that can't I?"

"Sure, why not, it's my name isn't it?

"I know, but things change over the years and, well, not sure if you got it changed, you know."

"No Ed, still the same, just me and my son, no man worthwhile has happened by yet that I can hook my claws into. Your still married to Mary right?"

"Yes I am and she told me not to get too friendly with ya, can you imagine that?"

"Smart woman that Mary, come on into the house, I just put a pot of coffee on the stove."

Sure would enjoy that," I said and in we went.

We had a good talk, I stayed the night giving her the clothes Mary asked me to give her, had a good man talk with her son James and left before daylight.

"Good folks, there Whiskey Gen, good folks, darn good cook too. Guess Mary and me doesn't have to worry anymore about her, as she is well looked after. Hope she gets a man though some day, too good a lookin' woman just to go to waste. Come on old girl, we got a lot of ground to cover today and all dry."

Took all morning to get to the desert and figured if lucky we would get to the watering hole mid way come dark, that is if things went right. Just as the sun was going down the water hole came into view

surrounded by some lush green grass, not much, but enough for Whiskey Gen to have a good meal.

I got down, took the saddle off and tied her under a tree, not that I thought she would run away on her own, but if some strange animal happened by one never knows; just couldn't take the chance.

In no time I was washed up and had coffee perkin' over a fire. Mary had fixed me enough ready made food for two days, which she figured with a meal at Jessica's place would be plenty. Right there and then I think I could have ate twice as much, her food being so tasty but I rationed myself.

I ate while chattin' to Whiskey Gen, then moved my saddle up against a rock near the fire, threw on a good size log and bedded down for the night.

The sky was clear and as I laid there, looking up at the sky my eyes laid on a million stars. Sure a sight to see I thought, I wonder what Mary is thinking right at this moment? Better be about me." Slowly my eyes closed, good night Mary and drifted off to sleep.

I was awakened by Whiskey Gen snorting as if to say come on now lets get a move on, can't be laying around here all day.

"OK old girl, I am awake and got up. In no time we were on our way, I didn't feel like taking the time for breakfast figuring I could eat in the saddle if the urge did hit.

About noon I sat up on a hill looking down at the town of Little Dixie Landing.

"Not much of a town huh Whiskey Gen? But I hear they have the best milking cows this side of Texas and that is what we came for."

I rode on into town stopping at the livery stable. Nice feller there, said he would put my horse in the barn, rub her down and feed her for five cents, which I thought was a bit high in price, but it was his barn.

I asked the fellow where I could find some cows to buy and he said he had a dozen or so out back of the barn for sale, two giving milk that are around two years old.

"Sounds like what I am looking for old timer, can we take a look?"

"Sure can, just wait a minute here till I unsaddle your horse and put her in a stall, she sure looks all in."

"Your right there, we did put a piece behind us today."

We then walked out behind the barn and sure enough there stood around fifteen of the nicest looking cows one could ever lay eyes on. I didn't want to seem too anxious in getting to the price part, so I just moseyed slowly on over to the corral talking about my trip here.

After a bit of chattin' the old feller I guess got tired of waiting and said, "I suppose you would like to know what I am selling them for?"

"Well it has entered my mind, I am sure there is lots of others around town I could look at." *But inside I knew these were fine animals.*

"So since you asked, what would you take for the two of them?"

"Well figured on getting' fifteen dollars each if I could." *Mary and me figured on twenty if they were really good but I wasn't about to tell him that.*

"Well, thing is old timer I only have twenty dollars on me, kind of was hoping I could get them for that an have enough for supper and a room for the night. I guess I will have to look around a bit, thanks anyways. They sure are nice cows though let me tell ya."

With that I turned and headed back to the barn.

"Hole up there now young feller, I didn't say I wouldn't sell you them cows for the price you said, I just said that was my asking price. Tell you what, you look like a nice feller, how about I sell you them there cows for ten dollars each and you come on over to our home and my wife will cook you supper. You can also sleep here in the barn, it's warm and good and dry and I will even throw in a blanket for the night."

I gotta' tell ya I was just a bustin' inside being so happy but held it in and said. "You got yourself a deal there my friend."

The night wore on, I ate well, lots of chatting was done about Mary, me and our farm, then said goodnight and headed on over to the barn to check on Whiskey Gen and get some sleep.

Morning came early. Walking out into the morning air I spotted a small General store off to one side of the street.

"Hmm, I do have some extra money left. I think I will go and buy some supplies along with a new red dress for Mary. She sure deserves it and I haven't seen her in a dress for, well, been a long long time."

The amazing thing was that a woman about Mary's size run the store, so I just asked her if she had a red dress that would fit her. She said yes I do and I told her to wrap it up.

Some apples, flour, salt, sugar, coffee and other things were bought that day with a new item called chocolates. Never heard of them before but the one the lady gave me to try was sure something to behold. Bought the whole box for one dollar. The most I ever paid for candy in my whole life.

We chatted some, while she was getting things done up, said thanks and headed on over to get Whiskey Gen, she is going to have a load going home I thought, maybe should have bought a pack horse. Worked out though, as I tied most of all the things onto the two cows. They didn't seem to mind, which was quite amazing I thought.

Soon I was on my way with two cows in tow. The trail seemed long and hot on the return trip, reason being I couldn't go as fast with the

two cows and supplies. Took an extra day, but we arrived in good spirits with me hollering from a half mile away.

"Where is that woman of mine, hope she didn't hook up with no whiskey salesman and leave me."

No more than a second later out of the cabin she came on the run. We both met halfway and I swung down just as she jumped into my arms.

"Got the cows Mary, oh....it's so good to see you."

We held each other for a few moments then slowly moved on toward the cabin, with me telling her all about the trip. The red dress was worn every Sunday after that, my she sure looked pretty. The two cows gave us many fine calf's and more milk than we could use.

That fall Mary brought into the world a boy which grew to be a fine fellow; went off to school and became a lawyer if you can believe that. We were sure proud let me tell ya.

Oh and them their chocolates, guess she must have liked them, as I only got one out of the whole box.

Helpful Hints-Bread Making. In bread making, as in baseball, there is nothing like a good batter in the hour of knead.

In Closing
I Would Like To Wish
You Well